Improving Your Spelling Skills

by Caleb E. Crowell

ISBN# 0-87694-218-4   EDI 388

Table of Contents

To the Student:

SPECIAL TIPS ON LEARNING HOW TO SPELL

This book is designed to help you improve your spelling skills. You will learn a fair number of spelling rules and some of the reasons for the rules. You will learn about the use of apostrophes, about capitalization, and about the use of the dictionary in finding out how to spell a word—even how to get around the problem of finding a word in the dictionary when you don't know how to spell it in the first place. At the end of the book there is a section that summarizes what you have learned and another section that tests you on what you have learned.

But learning the skills taught in this book will not make you a good speller unless you also train yourself to remember what you have learned. There is a special, 3-step way to do this. When you encounter a word whose spelling you want to learn, follow these steps:

1. **See the word in your mind.** First look at the word in written or printed form. Then close your eyes and imagine that you are looking at it on a chalkboard. Try to "see" it as a whole. Don't spell it letter by letter. See it.

2. **Say it the way it is spelled.** Many words are spelled very differently from the way they sound. If you want to learn how to spell a word like "Wednesday," it will help if you say it as "wed-nes-day," pronouncing every letter and splitting the word into 3 syllables. That's saying it the way it is spelled.

Saying a word the way it is spelled is especially helpful if you are learning to spell a word that contains the weak vowel sound known as a **schwa**. (For example, the last vowel sound in the word **vowel**, or the first vowel sound in the word **affect**.) Saying words like these the way they are spelled will help you distinguish words like **affect** and **effect**, which are actually pronounced the same in everyday speech but which are spelled differently and sound different when pronounced the way they are spelled. Saying a word the way it is spelled also helps you with a word like **independent**, which is often misspelled with an **-ant** at the end.

3. **Write the word.** This really helps, especially if you write it more than once. When your hand and mind have worked together to write a word correctly several times, you will be less apt to misspell it in the future.

As a final check, close your eyes again. Imagine you are writing the word on a chalkboard. Imagine not just how the word looks, but also the feel of writing it, of setting down each letter in order.

As you work through this book, follow this 3-step method. It works and it will be a useful method for you to know and use for the rest of your life.

PREFIXES & SUFFIXES

This section will introduce you to the basic spelling rules involved in adding a prefix or a suffix to a word.

Prefixes and suffixes are letter combinations like the *un–* in *unable* and the *–ly* in *nicely* that can be added to a word to change its meaning or its grammatical function. They are extremely important in English, since many of our most common words contain a prefix or a suffix. For example, here are some of the suffix–containing words in the first sentence on this page:

basic	*(base + -ic)*
involved	*(spell + -ing)*
rules	*(rule + -s)*
involved	*(involve + -ed)*
adding	*(add + -ing)*

As you will learn, adding a prefix to a word is almost never a spelling problem. However, many words change their spelling when certain suffixes or endings are added to them. This section will help you learn how to deal with most suffixes except *-s* and *-es* plural endings, which are the subject of the section in this series entitled *Plurals*.

1 Recognizing Prefixes, Suffixes and Base Words

In the English language, we often change the meaning or the grammatical function of a word by adding a letter or letter group to the beginning or end of the word. For example, look at these additions to the word *spell*:

> *mis*spell
> *re*spell
> spell*ing*
> spell*er*
> *un*spell*able*

Letter groups like *mis–* or *re–* that can be added to the beginning of a word are called **prefixes**. A prefix usually changes the meaning of a word.

Letter groups like *–ing* or *–er* that can be added to the end of a word are called **suffixes**. A suffix usually changes the grammatical function of a word. For example, the suffix *–er* changes the verb *spell* to the noun *speller*.

The word to which the prefix or suffix is added is called the **base** or **root**. Thus, a word like *unspellable* consists of the prefix *un–*, the base *spell*, and the suffix *–able*.

Many common spelling mistakes occur when certain prefixes or suffixes are added to certain base words. This book will show you how to avoid many of these mistakes. First, however, you should be able to recognize prefixes, suffixes, and bases when they occur in words you write. The exercises that follow will give you practice in doing this.

EXERCISES

Each of the following words consists of a base word plus a prefix. Write the base word in each example.

1. untie _____
2. replace _____
3. monoplane _____
4. distaste _____
5. superman _____

The following words all contain suffixes. Write the base of each word.

6. hardly _____
7. doing _____
8. rounded _____
9. doubtful _____
10. shipment _____

The following words may contain a prefix, a suffix, or both. Find the base of each word and write it.

11. selfish _____
12. prepayment _____
13. careless _____
14. replay _____
15. unknowing _____

When a suffix is added to a base, the spelling of the base sometimes changes. For example, when the suffix –*ful* is added to the base *beauty*, you get *beautiful*. The letter *y* changes to an *i*.

The spelling of the base of each of the following words changes when a suffix is added. Decide what the base of each word is and write it.

16. flier _____
17. reddish _____
18. valuable _____
19. hopping _____
20. hoping _____

ANSWERS

1. tie	7. do	14. play
2. place	8. round	15. know
3. plane	9. doubt	16. fly
4. taste	10. ship	17. red
5. man	11. self	18. value
6. hard	12. pay	19. hop
	13. care	20. hope

2 Spelling Problems with Prefixes and Suffixes

When a prefix is added to a base word, the spelling of both the prefix and the base remains unchanged:

un– + *happy* = *unhappy*
dis– + *agree* = *disagree*

Follow this rule even if the last letter of the prefix is the same as the first letter of the base:

dis– + *similar* = *dissimilar*
mis– + *spell* = *misspell*
co– + *operate* = *cooperate*

When certain suffixes are added to certain base words, however, the spelling of the base word may change in one of three ways:

A. The letter *y* may change to *i*:

lazy + –ly = lazily   busy + –ness = business

B. The letter *e* may be dropped:

hope + –ing = hoping   type + –ist = typist

C. The last letter of the base may be doubled:

hop + –ing = hopping   run + –er = runner

10

EXERCISES

Each of the following examples consists of a prefix plus a base word. After each one, write the word that results when you combine the prefix with the base.

1. sub– + marine _____
2. un– + necessary_____
3. over– + throw_____
4. dis– + service_____
5. pre– + judge_____

6. mis– + state_____
7. mis– + step _____
8. semi– + colon _____
9. in– + accurate _____

In each of the following sentences, find the word that contains a prefix. Look carefully at how it has been spelled. If it is misspelled, write the correct spelling. If it is already spelled correctly, write the letter C (for correct) after it.

10. Elena was disatisfied with the hotel._____
11. Admiral Grommet disliked the color of his ship._____
12. The Secretary of the Navy overode his order to paint the ship red. _____
13. Velma's great invention went unoticed._____
14. Is there a mispelled word in this sentence?_____

For the next exercises, refer to the listening at the bottom of the opposite page. The listing shows the three kinds of spelling changes that may occur in a base word when certain suffixes are added. Write the letter (A, B, or C) of the spelling change that has occurred in each of the following words.

15. letting _____
16. making _____
17. beginner_____
18. copier _____
19. sensible_____

ANSWERS

1. submarine
2. unnecessary
3. overthrow
4. disservice
5. prejudge
6. misstate
7. misstep
8. semicolon
9. inaccurate
10. dissatisfied
11. C
12. overrode
13. unnoticed
14. misspelled
15. C
16. B
17. C
18. A
19. B

3 Changing Y to I

When a suffix is added to certain words ending in the letter *y*, the *y* may change to an *i*. Whether it does or not depends on what the letter before the *y* is—a vowel or a consonant.

If the letter before the final *y* is a vowel (*a, e, i, o,* or *u*), the *y* usually does not change to an *i*:

> *annoy* + *–ed* = *annoyed* (The letter before the *y* is a vowel.)
> *pray* + *–ed* = *prayed* (The letter *a* is a vowel.)

But if the letter before the final *y* is a consonant (any letter except *a, e, i, o,* or *u*), the *y* changes to an *i*:

> *try* + *–ed* = *tried* (The letter before the *y* is a consonant.)
> *crazy* + *–ly* = *crazily* (The letter *z* is a consonant.)

Exceptions:

1. The *y* does not change to an *i* if the suffix already begins with an *i*. *Try* + *–ing* is not *triing*. It is *trying*.

2. *Shyness, dryness, slyness,* and *daily* are some of the exceptions to the rule. Remember them—particularly *daily*.

EXERCISES

In three of the following words, the final *y* changes to an *i* before a suffix (unless the suffix already begins with *i*.) Put a check mark before the numbers of these words. Leave the numbers of the others blank.

1. beauty   4. lazy
2. obey   5. heavy
3. journey

Now write the words formed by each of the following.

6. tardy + –ness _____
7. boy + –hood _____
8. glory + –ous _____
9. delay + –ed _____
10. employ + –ment _____

Suppose you are adding suffixes to words that end in a consonant plus *y*. Answer each of the following questions:

11. Will the *y* change to *i* if the suffix is –*er*? ☐ yes   ☐ no
12. Will the *y* change to *i* if the suffix is –*ness*? ☐ yes   ☐ no
13. Will the *y* change to *i* if the suffix is –*ing*? ☐ yes   ☐ no
14. Will the *y* change to *i* if the suffix is –*ist*? ☐ yes   ☐ no

Write the words formed by each of the following:

15. copy + –er _____
16. copy + –ist _____
17. delay + –ing _____
18. bury + –al _____
19. slay + –er _____
20. day + –ly (Be careful of this one. It's an exception.) _____

13

ANSWERS

1. ✔
2. (blank)
3. (blank)
4. ✔
5. ✔
6. tardiness
7. boyhood
8. glorious
9. delayed
10. employment
11. yes
12. yes
13. no
14. no
15. copier
16. copyist
17. delaying
18. burial
19. slayer
20. daily

4 Dropping the Final E

Many English words end with the letter *e*. Usually this letter is **silent**—it is not pronounced, although it often changes the pronunciation of a vowel that comes earlier in the word. Notice the difference in the way you pronounce *hop* and *hope*, or *hid* and *hide*, to see the difference a final silent *e* can make.

Final *e* is usually dropped before a suffix that begins with a vowel:

> *move* + *-ing* = *moving*
> *move* + *-er* = *mover*
> *move* + *-able* = *movable*

> **BUT:** *move* + *-ment* = *movement* (The suffix does *not* begin with a vowel. It begins with a consonant. So the *e* is kept.)

> **COMMON EXCEPTIONS:** *truly, argument*

When a *c* or a *g* comes before the final *e*, as in *notice* and *courage*, the rule is a little different. In words like these, the final *e* is dropped only before suffixes beginning with *e* or *i*.

Here are examples of words with *ge* endings.

> *manage* + *-er* = *manager*   *manage* + *-ing* = *managing*

BUT: *manage + –able = manageable* ⎫ Suffix does not
manage + –ment = management ⎭ begin with *e* or *i*.

COMMON EXCEPTIONS: *judgment, acknowledgment*

The examples would be similar for a word with a *ce* ending:

notice + –ing = noticing   **BUT** *notice + –able = noticeable*

EXERCISES

Write the words formed by each of the following. (Hint: look at the first letter of the suffix and then decide if the final *e* should be dropped from the base word.)

1. leave + –ing _____
2. ride + –er _____
3. time + –ly _____
4. remove + –al _____
5. loose + –ness _____

The base words in the following exercises end in *ce* or *ge*. Write the words formed by each combination of base and suffix.

6. age + –ing _____
7. peace + –able _____
8. peace + –ful _____
9. voice + –ed _____
10. outrage + –ous _____

Write the words formed by each of the following. Be careful of base words ending in *ce* and *ge*.

11. value + –able _____
12. change + –able _____
13. revise + –ion _____
14. piece + –ing _____
15. hope + –ful _____

Before you forget, here are combinations of suffixes added to words ending in *y*. (If you are not sure of the rules, turn back to the two previous pages. And watch out for exceptions.) Write the words formed by each:

16. day + –ly _____
17. try + –al _____
18. buy + –er _____
19. dry + –ing _____

ANSWERS

1. leaving
2. rider
3. timely
4. removal
5. looseness
6. aging
7. peaceable
8. peaceful
9. voiced
10. outrageous
11. valuable
12. changeable
13. revision
14. piecing
15. hopeful
16. daily
17. trial
18. buyer
19. drying

5 Doubling the Final Consonant: One-Syllable Words

Many English words end with the following letter combination: **consonant-vowel-consonant** (**CVC** for short). Here are a few:

chin	*label*	*dolphin*	*run*
swim	*slap*	*permit*	*dot*

Look at the last three letters in the above examples. They all end with CVC.

One-syllable words with the CVC ending double the final consonant before a suffix that begins with a vowel. For example:

chin + *–ing* = *chinning*   Suffix begins with a vowel.
glad + *–en* = *gladden*   Double the final consonant.

glad + *–ly* = *gladly*   Suffix begins with a consonant.
glad + *–ness* = *gladness*   No doubling.

Be careful to double the final consonant *only* when the word ends with CVC. Each of the following words ends with a consonant, but not with CVC. Therefore, the final consonant would *not* be doubled before any suffix:

teach (ends VCC):   *teach* + *–ing* = *teaching*
read (ends VVC):   *read* + *–ing* = *reading*
search (ends CCC):   *search* + *–ing* = *searching*

EXCEPTION: The letter *x* is really a combination of two consonant sounds—*k* and *s*. Do not double it. *Mix* + *–ing* is *mixing*, not *mixxing*.

EXERCISES

Place a check mark by the number of any of the following words that would double the final consonant before a suffix beginning with a vowel. Leave the others blank. (Remember the test: CVC.)

1. church _____   4. walk_____
2. prod _____   5. fix (Be careful. It's an exception.)
3. wed _____   _____
                                  6. hop_____

All base words in the following exercises end with CVC. Write the words formed by each combination of base and suffix. (Hint: is the first letter of the suffix a vowel or a consonant?)

7. red + –ish _____   10. cup + –ful_____
8. war + –ing _____   11. mix + –er_____
9. bad + –ly_____

Each base word in the following exercises ends with a consonant. Write the words formed by each combination of base plus suffix. (Warning: some of the base words do not end with CVC.)

12. act + –ion_____   15. rob + –er_____
13. stop + –ed_____   16. chin + –ing_____
14. float + –er_____   17. lid + –less _____

18. knot + –ing_____
19. fix + –er_____
20. short + –ly_____

ANSWERS

1. (blank)	7. reddish	14. floater
2. ✔	8. warring	15. robber
3. ✔	9. badly	16. chinning
4. (blank)	10. cupful	17. lidless
5. (blank)	11. mixer	18. knotting
6. ✔	12. action	19. fixer
	13. stopped	20. shortly

6 Doubling the Final Consonant: Words of More Than One Syllable

On the last two pages, you learned to double the final consonant of a one-syllable CVC word before a suffix beginning with a vowel. What about words with more than one syllable? Look at these examples:

alter + *–ing* = *altering* (no doubling)
prefer + *–ing* = *preferring* (doubling)
prefer + *–ence* = *preference* (no doubling)

Here's the rule:

Pronounce the word with the suffix added, and notice which syllable is stressed. If the stress falls on the last syllable of the base word, the final consonant is doubled. For example:

prefer + *–ing* = *prefer͟ring* (double consonant)
prefer + *–ed* = *prefer͟red* (double consonant)
BUT:
prefer + *–ence* = *pref͟erence* (do *not* double consonant)
alter + *–ing* = *al͟tering* (do *not* double consonant)

Remember that, for this rule to apply, the word must end with CVC and the suffix must begin with a vowel.

18

EXERCISES

Each of the following base words ends with CVC; the suffixes all begin with vowels. Write the words formed by each combination. Remember —pronounce the word first before you decide whether or not to double the consonant.

1. omit + –ing _____
2. forget + –ing _____
3. open + –er _____
4. commit + –ed _____
5. listen + –er _____

Each of the following base words ends with CVC. Some of the suffixes begin with consonants. Write the words formed by each combination. Be sure to pronounce the word *and* check to see what kind of letter the suffix begins with before you decide whether to double the final consonant.

6. confer + –ence _____
7. confer + –ing _____
8. forget + –ful _____
9. forget + –ing _____
10. sudden + –ly _____

Write the words formed by each combination below. Be careful— some of the long words do *not* end with CVC.

11. consider + –ation _____
12. refer + –al _____
13. refer + –ence _____
14. confirm + –ing _____
15. appoint + –ing _____
16. appear + –ed _____
17. occur + –ence _____
18. suspect + –ing _____
19. maroon + –ed _____

ANSWERS

1. omitting
2. forgetting
3. opener
4. committed
5. listener
6. conference
7. conferring
8. forgetful
9. forgetting
10. suddenly
11. consideration
12. referral
13. reference
14. confirming
15. appointing
16. appeared
17. occurrence
18. suspecting
19. marooned

7 Review of Prefixes and Suffixes

Here is a review of the spelling rules you have learned in this section:

When Adding a Prefix:

1. Write the prefix and the base word together. There is no spelling change even if the last letter of the prefix and the first letter of the base word are the same.

When Adding a Suffix:

1. Change final *y* to *i* if the *y* is preceded by a consonant, unless the suffix already begins with an *i*.
2. Drop final silent *e* before suffixes beginning with a vowel; if the base word ends with *ce* or *ge*, drop the *e* only before suffixes beginning with *e* or *i*.
3. Double the final consonant of words ending with CVC before suffixes beginning with a vowel, if the last syllable of the base word is stressed when the suffix is added. Exception: words ending with *x* or *w*.

EXERCISES

Write the words formed by the following combinations of prefix and base:

1. un– + happy_____
2. un– + necessary_____
3. mis– + spell _____
4. mis– + place _____
5. re– + elect_____

Write the words formed by the following combinations of suffixes with words ending with the letter *y*.

6. annoy + –ance_____
7. employ + –ed_____
8. employ + –ment_____
9. apply + –ing_____
10. juicy + –ly_____

Write the words formed by the following combinations of suffixes with words ending with a silent *e*.

11. decide + –ing_____
12. grace + –ful_____
13. encourage + –ed_____
14. explore + –ation_____
15. move + –ment_____

Write the words formed by the following combinations of suffixes with words ending with CVC.

16. pad + –ed_____
17. exit + –ing_____
18. begin + –er_____
19. wit + –less_____
20. prefer + –ence_____

Here is a mixture of various kinds of base words and suffixes. Write the words formed by each combination:

21. play + –ful_____
22. box + –er_____
23. discourage + –ing_____
24. blue + –ish_____
25. decide + –ing_____
26. pat + –ing_____
27. nice + –ly_____
28. beauty + –cian_____
29. perform + –ance_____
30. grim + –ly_____

ANSWERS

1. unhappy
2. unnecessary
3. misspell
4. misplace
5. reelect
6. annoyance
7. employed
8. employment
9. applying
10. juicily
11. deciding
12. graceful
13. encouraged
14. exploration
15. movement
16. padded
17. exiting
18. beginner
19. witless
20. preference
21. playful
22. boxer
23. discouraging
24. bluish
25. deciding
26. patting
27. nicely
28. beautician
29. performance
30. grimly

B
PLURALS

As you know, the plural form of most nouns is formed by adding the suffix –s to the singular form. However, many words add an –es instead. Some words change their spelling before adding an –s or –es. Some words have irregular plurals. And some have a plural form that is the same as the singular.

This section will show you how to form and spell all these kinds of plurals. It will also show you how to spell the -s form of the present tense of a verb, which is formed in many cases like the plural of a noun.

⑧ Plurals with -S and -ES

The plural of most English nouns is formed by adding –s to the singular:

dog—dogs	finger—fingers	table—tables
pig—pigs	mountain—mountains	ear—ears

However, if the singular ends in s, z, ch, sh, or x, the plural is formed by adding –es to the singular:

boss—bosses	church—churches	fox—foxes
buzz—buzzes	rash—rashes	

This is as much a pronunciation rule as a spelling rule. If you pronounce s, z, ch, sh, and x, you will notice that they all contain hissing or shushing sounds. It would be difficult to pronounce the plural of a word ending in these sounds if just an –s were added.

Try it. Pronounce these imaginary plurals just as they are written:

bosss	churchs	foxs
buzzs	rashs	

You will find that you can barely pronounce them, or that the final –s is blurred and not distinct. For this reason, –es is the plural ending for words whose singular ends in a hissing or shushing sound. Of course, if such a word ends with a silent e, you need only add an –s to make it plural—although you pronounce the e when you say the plural:

mustache—mustaches   bruise—bruises

These spelling rules for adding –s or –es to words also apply to verb forms in the present tense:

I see, he sees	I miss, he misses
I walk, she walks	I clutch, Bill clutches

EXERCISES

Write the plural form of each of the following nouns:

1. latch _____
2. wallet _____
3. ocean _____
4. mesh _____
5. six _____
6. kiss _____
7. sea _____
8. conversation _____
9. piece _____
10. ditch _____

Write the correct present tense form of the verb in parentheses in each of the following sentences.

11. Admiral Grommet (wish) to send the entire fleet around the world.
_____

12. He (think) it will improve the morale of the sailors. _____

13. He himself (refuse) to go, of course. _____

14. A long voyage (make) him seasick. _____

15. He (propose) to fly to the ports that the ships will visit.
_____

16. Susan (catch) fish using only a bent pin. _____

17. She never (miss) a chance to talk about all the fish she has caught.
_____

ANSWERS

1. latches
2. wallets
3. oceans
4. meshes
5. sixes
6. kisses
7. seas
8. conversations
9. pieces
10. ditches
11. wishes
12. thinks
13. refuses
14. makes
15. proposes
16. catches
17. misses

⑨ Words Ending in Y and O

There are special rules for spelling the plurals of certain nouns ending in *y* or *o*.

If the letter before the *y* or *o* is a vowel (*a, e, i, o,* or *u*), there is no problem. Simply add an –*s* to form the plural:

boy—boys   *day—days*
cameo—cameos   *boo—boos*

If the letter before the *y* or *o* is a consonant, however, the plurals follow special rules.

To spell the plural of a noun ending in a consonant plus *y*, change the *y* to an *i* and add –*es*:

try—tries   *pony—ponies*

There is really no useful guide or rule for spelling the plural of nouns ending in a consonant plus *o*. Some are spelled by adding –*es*:

potato—potatoes   *echo—echoes*

Others simply add an –*s*. (Most proper nouns and musical terms ending in a consonant plus *o* form their plurals in this way.) For example:

Filipino—Filipinos   *banjo—banjos*   *silo—silos*

To make matters complicated, many can be spelled either way:

zeros **or** *zeroes*   *mosquitos* **or** *mosquitoes*

In the following exercises, the words that end in a consonant plus *o* are words which form their plurals by adding *–es,* except for proper nouns and musical terms. Remember, however, that when you write these plurals, you will often have to consult a dictionary.

EXERCISES

Write the plurals of the following nouns ending in *y.* Remember to check whether the *y* is preceded by a consonant or a vowel.

1. lady _____
2. donkey _____
3. duty _____
4. country _____
5. delay _____
6. army _____
7. monkey _____

Write the plurals of the following nouns ending in *o.* Remember to check whether the letter before the *o* is a consonant or a vowel, and whether the word is a proper noun or a musical term.

8. veto _____
9. piano _____
10. portfolio _____
11. tomato _____
12. soprano _____
13. radio _____
14. hero _____
15. rodeo _____

10 Words Ending in F or FE

Nouns that end in *f* or *f* plus a silent *e* (*knife*, for example) may form their plurals in one of two ways.

Some, like *belief*, merely add an *–s*: *beliefs*.

Others change the *f* or *fe* to a *v* and add an *–es*:

    wife—wives   *knife—knives*

There is no spelling rule that can tell you which way the plural of a particular word ending in *f* or *fe* is formed. You have to know how it is pronounced before you will know how to spell it. In most cases you already possess this knowledge. You knew before you picked up this book, for example, that the plural of *knife* contains a *v* sound.

A few words, like *dwarf*, *hoof*, and *scarf*, can form their plurals either way—*dwarfs* or *dwarves*, *hoofs* or *hooves*, *scarfs* or *scarves*. If you are in doubt, consult a dictionary.

EXERCISES

Write the plurals of the following nouns ending in *f* or *fe*. **Be sure to pronounce the plural before you write it.**

1. life _____
2. chief _____
3. sniff _____
4. half _____
5. gulf _____

Before you forget, write the plural of the following nouns ending in *o* and *y*. If you are not sure of the rules, turn back and review them.

6. city _____
7. play _____
8. sympathy _____
9. cuckoo _____
10. potato _____

ANSWERS

1. lives
2. chiefs
3. sniffs
4. halves
5. gulfs
6. cities
7. plays
8. sympathies
9. cuckoos
10. potatoes

11 Irregular Plurals

A small number of English nouns have irregular plurals. That is, their plurals are not formed by adding –s or –es to the singular. Here are the singular forms of some of these nouns:

man	*tooth*	*goose*
woman	*foot*	*ox*
child	*mouse*	*louse*

You probably know the plurals of most or all of these words. In any case, you will have a chance to test yourself in the exercises that follow.

A few other words have the same form in the plural that they have in the singular:

deer	*salmon*	*fish*
trout	*moose*	*Sioux* (the Indian tribe)

Most of these words are the names of animals or fish.

EXERCISES

Write the plurals of the following nouns:

1. man _____
2. woman _____
3. child _____
4. tooth _____
5. foot _____
6. mouse _____
7. goose _____
8. ox _____
9. louse _____
10. sheep _____

12 Symbols, Proper Names, and Compound Nouns

Symbols, such as individual letters, numbers, and special signs, are made plural by adding an apostrophe plus –s:

The word "aardvark" begins with two **a's**.
The blackboard was covered with +**'s**, –**'s**, *and other mathematical signs.*
Three **9's** *make 27.*

The plural of a word considered purely as a word is formed the same way:

You have too many **and's** *in that sentence.*

The plural of a proper name—for example, the *Joneses* (meaning the Jones family)—is formed by adding –s or –es without regard to the special cases of words ending in *y, o, f,* or *fe.* Thus, Mr. and Mrs. *Wolf* are the *Wolfs,* even though the ordinary plural of *wolf* is *wolves.*

Compound nouns, such as *brother-in-law* or *maid of honor* usually form the plural by making plural the most important part of the compound:

brothers-in-law   *step-children*
maids of honor

Note the following exceptions:

ten-year-olds   *drive-ins*

EXERCISES

Write the plurals of the following symbols.

1. + _____
2. 6 _____
3. 1,000 _____
4. h _____
5. – _____

Write the plural of the item in parentheses in each of the following sentences.

6. The (Littlecalf) left their house. _____
7. The (calf) were separated from the rest of the herd. _____
8. Lucy was still unsure of her (ABC). _____
9. Frederick wished he was living in the (1400). _____
10. Maria is the only pupil I have ever seen who spells the word "Mississippi" with too many (s). _____
11. Duke Otto always kept two (guard of honor) standing at attention by his chair. _____
12. Entering a classroom filled with (seven-year-old) is a terrifying experience. _____
13. The students organized (sit-in) in the cafeteria to protest about the food. _____

13 Adding -S and -ES to Verbs

Most verbs in English have two present tense forms—one identical with the root and one with an –s or –es ending added to the root.

The rules for spelling the –s or –es form of a verb are very similar to those for spelling the plurals of nouns:

run:	He runs.
teach:	She teaches. (word ending is s, z, ch, sh, or x)
say:	He says. (word ending in vowel plus y)
try:	She tries. (word ending in consonant plus y)
radio:	He radios. (word ending in vowel plus o)
go:	She goes. (word ending in consonant plus o)

Verbs ending in f or fe do not, however, change their endings to –ves as some nouns do. They merely add an –s. For example, take the word knife:

She had two knives.	(knife used as a noun)
She knifes through the water.	(knife used as a verb)

Many nouns ending in f or fe have corresponding verb forms ending in ve: belief (noun), believe (verb). In cases like this, the verb still follows the regular rule: He believes.

Similarly, if a word like *man* is used as a verb, *-s* is added to make any present tense form different from the root.

He saw two *men*.   (*man* used as a noun)
He *mans* the lifeboat.   (*man* used as a verb)

EXERCISES

Write the correct present tense form of the verb in parentheses in each of the following sentences.

1. At times Roberta (notice) more than she should. _____
2. My three-year-old sister (smash) every toy she gets. _____
3. Naturally, she (do) not have any toys left. _____
4. So now she (destroy) things belonging to me. _____
5. Duke Otto (reply) rudely to anything you say to him. _____
6. His voice (echo) across the canyon. _____

In the following sentences, choose the correct form of the word in parentheses and copy it.

7. Roger (wolfs, wolves) his food down at every meal. _____
8. Many men have died for their (beliefs, believes). _____
9. Eleanor (griefs, grieves) over her lost opportunities. _____
10. Throw him to the (wolfs, wolves). _____
11. Frederick firmly (beliefs, believes) that the world is flat as a pancake. _____

ANSWERS

1. notices
2. smashes
3. does
4. destroys
5. replies
6. echoes
7. wolfs
8. beliefs
9. grieves
10. wolves
11. believes

14 Review of Spelling Plurals

Here is a review of the main points about spelling plurals discussed in this book.

1. As a general rule, add –s to a noun to form its plural: *dog, dogs.*

2. If the noun ends in *s, z, sh, ch,* or *x,* add –es to form the plural: *boss, bosses.*

3. If the noun ends in a consonant + *y,* change *y* to *i* and add –es: *baby, babies.*

4. Many nouns ending with a consonant + *o* form plurals by adding –es; others, particularly proper nouns and nouns having to do with music, add an –s: *potato, potatoes; solo, solos; Eskimo, Eskimos.*

5. Certain nouns ending in *f* or *fe* change the *f* or *fe* ending to a *v* and add –es: *wolf, wolves.*

6. A few nouns have irregular plurals or plurals which have the same form as the singular. These must be memorized.

7. Symbols, such as letters and numbers, add an apostrophe plus –s to form the plural: *4, 4's.*

8. Compound nouns usually pluralize the most important part of the compound: *sister-in-law, sisters-in-law.*

9. The –s or –es present tense form of most verbs is formed like the plural of a noun, except that rules 5 and 6, above, do not apply to verbs.

EXERCISES

Write the plurals of the following nouns.

1. belief_____
2. fox_____
3. ox_____
4. mustache_____
5. catch_____
6. lady_____
7. day_____
8. child_____
9. tomato_____
10. wife_____
11. piece_____
12. man-at-arms_____
13. eye_____
14. fish_____
15. mesh_____
16. sheep_____
17. half_____
18. company_____
19. soprano_____
20. duty_____
21. 9_____
22. miss_____
23. Wolf (a family name—Mr. and Mrs. Wolf)_____

Choose the correct present tense form of each verb in parentheses and write it in the blanks.

24. He (relaxs, relaxes) after every meal._____
25. She (beliefs, believes) what you say._____
26. He (mans, men) the oars._____
27. She (wolfs, wolves) down her food._____
28. He (gos, goes) home._____

ANSWERS

1. beliefs
2. foxes
3. oxen
4. mustaches
5. catches
6. ladies
7. days
8. children
9. tomatoes
10. wives
11. pieces
12. men-at-arms
13. eyes
14. fish
15. meshes
16. sheep
17. halves
18. companies
19. sopranos
20. duties
21. 9's
22. misses
23. Wolfs
24. relaxes
25. believes
26. mans
27. wolfs
28. goes

C

IE & EI

Many words in English contain the letter combination *ie* or *ei*—for example, *piece, science, neighbor,* and *height.* It is often hard to remember, however, whether a particular word is spelled with an *ie* or an *ei*. This short section will teach you the standard rules for spelling such words, and the exceptions to the rules.

15 Put I Before E, Except After C

There is a simple rhyme that will tell you how to spell most words that contain the letter combination *ie* or *ei*. The first part of the rhyme is:

Put *i* before *e*,
Except after *c*.

Examples of the first line of the rhyme are:

believe   *quiet*   *handkerchief*

The order is reversed after the letter *c*. After *c*, the letter *e* comes before *i*:

deceive   *receipt*   *conceit*

Of course, to use this rhyme, you must first know that a word contains an *ei* or an *ie* letter combination. If you think that *believe* is spelled *beleve* or *beleeve*, the rhyme cannot help you. You will find in most cases, however, that you are familiar with many common *ie* and *ei* words. If you remember the rhyme, you will spell them correctly.

EXERCISES

Each of the following words contains the letter combination *ie* or *ei* in the space marked by the dashes. Decide for each word whether it should be spelled with an *ie* or an *ei*. Then write the entire word.

1. ch——f _____
2. d——t _____
3. th——f _____
4. rec——ver _____
5. n——ce _____
6. br——f _____
7. f——ld _____
8. fr——ndliness _____
9. conc——t _____
10. c——ling _____

ANSWERS
1. chief
2. diet
3. thief
4. receiver
5. niece
6. brief
7. field
8. friendliness
9. conceit
10. ceiling

16 Or When Sounded Like A

You have just learned the first part of the *"ie"* rhyme. The complete rhyme is:

Put *i* before *e*
Except after *c*,
Or when sounded like *a*
As in *neighbor* and *weigh*.

As the last two lines of the rhyme suggest, when the vowel combination is pronounced as in *neighbor* and *weigh,* the e goes before the i.

If you have not memorized this rhyme, do so now before you go on to the exercises. When you think you have it memorized, look away from this book and try saying it to yourself. And be sure you know what the rhyme means.

When you have memorized the rhyme, go on to the exercises on the next page.

EXERCISES

The list below contains examples of *ie* and *ei* words. As you did in the previous set of exercises, copy the words, supplying the missing letters. Follow the rules of the rhyme. As a check on your spelling, pronounce each word after you have written it.

1. fr——ght _____
2. rec——ve _____
3. misch——f _____
4. f——ry _____
5. ——ght _____
6. p——ce _____
7. r——gn _____
8. w——ght _____
9. cash——r _____
10. v——l _____

ANSWERS
1. freight   6. piece
2. receive   7. reign
3. mischief   8. weight
4. fiery   9. cashier
5. eight   10. veil

17 Exceptions and Review

There are certain exceptions to the *ie—ei* rule of the spelling rhyme. Many are contained in this sentence—which unfortunately makes very little sense:

Neither leisured foreign sheik seized their weird height.

Learn this sentence. All the words in it are spelled *ei*, as are similar words like *either* (the opposite of *neither*).

There are a few additional exceptions: *protein, forfeit, heifer* (a young cow), and the names *Sheila* and *Neil*.

All of these exceptions appear in the following expanded version of the sentence:

Neither leisured foreign sheik seized their weird height as forfeit for their heifer's protein, O Sheila and Neil.

Perhaps you can construct a better sentence, although you should have a lot of spare time on your hands before you try. For now, however, memorize the sentence as it appears on the page.

Exceptions to the rule of *ei* after *c* appear in the following sentence, which you should also learn:

A financier is a species of scientist.

The key words in this sentence, and other words they suggest (such as *science*), are spelled with an *ie* after the letter *c*.

Before you go on to the exercises, see if you can recite to yourself the three items you have memorized:

the four-line rhyme
the sentence with exceptions to *i* before *e* (*ei* words)
the sentence with exceptions to *ei* after *c* (*cie* words)

When you have memorized all three, go on to the exercises.

Look at the words below. In the blank spaces in each word, write *ie* or *ei*, whichever is correct.

1. fr——nd_____
2. gr——ving_____
3. n——ghbor_____
4. th——r_____
5. rel——ved_____
6. for——gn_____
7. dec——ver_____
8. h——ght_____
9. w——ght_____
10. br——fly_____

11. ——ghty_____
12. ——ther_____
13. bel——ver_____
14. v——l_____
15. rec——ve_____
16. s——ze_____
17. sc——nce_____
18. f——ld_____
19. w——rd_____
20. conc——ted_____

ANSWERS

1. friend
2. grieving
3. neighbor
4. their
5. relieved
6. foreign
7. deceiver
8. height
9. weight
10. briefly
11. eighty
12. either
13. believer
14. veil
15. receive
16. seize
17. science
18. field
19. weird
20. conceited

D

HOMOPHONES

Homophones (sometimes called *homonyms*) are words that are pronounced similarly but spelled differently—*bare* and *bear*, for example. They cause spelling problems when you mean to write one but write the other by mistake. A sentence like *We saw a brown bare* contains a spelling mistake caused by confusion of homophones.

There are hundreds of homophones in English. This section compares many of the most common ones. In addition, it compares other words that are not, strictly speaking, homophones, but that are often confused—such as *loose* and *lose*.

18 Homophones Containing a Long Vowel

Many spelling problems with homophones occur because English has so many ways to spell the sounds of **long vowels** (the vowel sounds in *mate*, *meet*, *mite*, *mote*, and *mute*). For example, say each of the following words to yourself:

meet   seize   chief   Pete   heat

All these words are pronounced with the same long vowel sound—long *e*. But the sound is spelled five different ways.

Below are some common pairs of homophones. All but the last two cause problems because they spell the same long vowel in two different ways. The last two pairs also contain long vowels, but the spelling confusion is caused by the other letters. Look carefully at the spelling and meaning of each word in each pair.

brake	The device that stops a car or a machine.
break	To smash or crack.
stake	A post pointed at one end.
steak	A piece of beef.
steel	A kind of metal.
steal	To take by theft.
week	Seven days.
weak	Not strong.
plain	Ordinary. Also, a region of level ground.
plane	An airplane. Also, a woodworking tool.
waste	To throw away something without using it.
waist	The part of the body just above the hips.
real	True or actual.
reel	Something you can wind string on.

die	(past tense, *died*). To stop living.
dye	(past tense, *dyed*). To color, or a color.
right	Correct. Also, the opposite of *left*.
write	To put words on paper.
whole	Complete.
hole	An empty space.

Study these homophones. Try to memorize the spelling and meaning of each one before you go on to the exercises.

EXERCISES

Look over each of the following sentences. In each sentence, choose the word in parentheses that fits the meaning of the sentence and underline it.

1. Don't (waste, waist) your food.
2. Lucas waited a (week, weak) for the blowgun to arrive.
3. Mrs. Rodriguez fishes with a rod, a (real, reel), and a hook.
4. Frederick spent the whole day making paper (plains, planes).
5. Selecting a doughnut, he gazed through the (hole, whole).
6. I hope your answers are (right, write).
7. Jane managed to (steel, steal) an entire buffalo herd.
8. She dined on buffalo (stake, steak) for a year.
9. Spotting ice, the driver stepped on the (break, brake).
10. Betty wrote a (hole, whole) play in an evening.
11. Below the mountains, a (plain, plane) stretched far away.
12. We marked the location of the treasure with a (steak, stake).
13. Julius has a slim (waste, waist).
14. If Mr. Galt sits on that couch, he'll (brake, break) it.
15. Please (right, write) words people can read.
16. Nelson felt (week, weak) as a kitten.
17. Bridges are often made of (steel, steal).
18. Are those diamonds (reel, real)?
19. Marcia (died, dyed) the cloth dark blue.
20. The old horse finally (died, dyed).
21. Mr. Nomura seemed to be a (plain, plane) simple man.

ANSWERS

1. waste	8. steak	15. write
2. week	9. brake	16. weak
3. reel	10. whole	17. steel
4. planes	11. plain	18. real
5. hole	12. stake	19. dyed
6. right	13. waist	20. died
7. steal	14. break	21. plain

19 Confusing Unaccented Syllables

In English, the vowel sound in an unaccented syllable often tends to have a sound somewhat like the *u* in *but*, no matter what its spelling is. For example, the word *affectionate*, which contains every vowel except *u*, is often pronounced something like *uh-FEK-shun-ut*. Thus, it is hard to know how to spell a word with one or more unaccented syllables just from hearing it. You have to see it written. The words below are a selection of homophones that sound alike because of the pronunciation of the unaccented syllable.

affect	To influence. (verb)
effect	An influence or result. (noun)
accept	To receive willingly.
except	Besides, or but. (preposition)
capital	The town or city where a state or country's government is.
capitol	The building in the capital where the lawmakers meet.
miner	A worker in a mine.
minor	Less important. Also, someone under 18 or 21.

principal	Most important. Also, the head of a school.
principle	A moral or scientific rule.
stationary	Not moving.
stationery	Paper for writing letters.

As you did before, study these homophones. Try to memorize the spelling and meaning of each before you go on to the exercises.

EXERCISES

For each sentence, choose the word in parentheses that best fits the meaning of the sentence and underline it.

1. Nothing you say will (affect, effect) him.
2. Nothing you say will have an (affect, effect) on him.
3. The streets of the (capital, capitol) were lined with trees.
4. Rivers illustrate the (principal, principle) that water flows downhill.
5. Pick up some pencils at the (stationary, stationery) store.
6. It was only a (miner, minor) problem, easily solved.
7. The teacher did not want to (accept, except) Marlene's gift of a tarantula spider.
8. Animals move, but plants are (stationary, stationery).
9. We all confessed (accept, except) Sue.
10. The (principal, principle) shuddered when Frederick walked in.
11. The dome of the (capital, capitol) glittered in the sunlight.
12. He had been a coal (miner, minor) for over forty years.
13. The (principal, principle) reason for the disturbance was Marvin's desire to restage the Boston Tea Party in every detail.

ANSWERS

1. affect
2. effect
3. capital
4. principle
5. stationery
6. minor

7. accept
8. stationary
9. except
10. principal
11. capitol
12. miner
13. principal

20 Homophones for Some People, Not for Others

People pronounce words differently in different parts of the country. For example, in many regions the first syllable of the word *forest* is pronounced like *far*. In other regions it is pronounced like *for*.

For this reason, there are some groups of words that are homophones for some people but not for others. Some of these words and their definitions appear below, together with other words that might be confused with them.

formerly	In the past.
formally	In a strict and proper manner.
quite	Fairly, or rather. (modifies adjectives)
quiet	Silent. (adjective)
quit	To stop.
whether	If.
weather	Sunshine, rain, or cloudiness. (noun)
than	A word used in making comparisons.
then	At that time. (adverb)
clothes	What people wear.
close	(when the *s* has a *z* sound). To shut.

close	(when the *s* has an *s* sound). Near.
cloths	The plural of the word *cloth*.
poor	Not rich. Also, not good quality.
pour	To empty out in a stream.
pore	A small hole in the skin through which we sweat.

EXERCISES

In each sentence, underline the word in parentheses that best fits the meaning of the sentence.

1. Don't you know when to (quite, quiet, quit)?
2. Don't you know when to be (quite, quiet, quit)?
3. It looks like stormy (whether, weather) tonight.
4. Doris mopped up the water with two (clothes, close, cloths).
5. He was sweating from every (poor, pour, pore).
6. First my father tried reasoning with me; (than, then) he tried shouting.
7. The hippopotamus came too (clothes, close, cloths) for comfort.
8. The king bowed (formerly, formally).
9. I don't know (weather, whether) or not I want to go.
10. Admiral Grommet was (quite, quiet, quit) annoyed.
11. Frederick wouldn't believe that Mount Everest was taller (than, then) Stone Hill.
12. Please (clothes, close, cloths) the door.
13. Millionaire Hendrix always pretends that he's (poor, pour, pore).
14. He was (formerly, formally) an office boy; now he's the president.
15. Lynn was wearing work (clothes, close, cloths).
16. Vincent started to (poor, pour, pore) salt in his coffee.
17. That is a very (poor, pour, pour) excuse, Kathy.

ANSWERS

1. quit	7. close	13. poor
2. quiet	8. formally	14. formerly
3. weather	9. whether	15. clothes
4. cloths	10. quite	16. pour
5. pore	11. than	17. poor
6. then	12. close	

21 Confusing Spellings

There are a number of verbs whose root forms are often confused with their past tense forms or with another word that has a similar spelling. For example, many people get confused when they spell the word pronounced *looz*—they aren't sure whether to write it *loose* or *lose*.

Here are examples of words that cause this kind of confusion:

choose   (rhymes with *ooze*). To make a choice—present tense.
chose   (rhymes with *nose*). Past tense of *choose*.

loose   (rhymes with *goose*). Not tight; free.
lose   (rhymes with *ooze*). To misplace and not find again.

advise   (rhymes with *rise*—the *s* has a *z* sound). To suggest. (verb)
advice   (rhymes with *rice*—the *c* has an *s* sound). A suggestion. (noun)

lead   (rhymes with *bead*). To go first or to show the way. (verb)
lead   (rhymes with *head*). A heavy metal. (noun)
led   Past tense of the verb *lead*.

passed   Past tense of the verb *pass*.
past   Gone by. (adjective)

desert	(accent on first syllable). A dry empty region. (noun)
desert	(accent on last syllable). To leave. (verb)
dessert	(accent on last syllable). Something sweet at the end of a meal.

EXERCISES

In each example, underline the word in parentheses that best fits the meaning of the sentence.

1. He gave us very bad (advice, advise).
2. I've needed someone to (lead, led) us through the swamp.
3. Cactus grows in the (desert, dessert).
4. Your shoelace is (loose, lose).
5. By mistake, Frederick's name (lead, led) the rest.
6. It is not easy to (choose, chose) between homonyms.
7. Fifteen minutes (passed, past) before anyone spoke.
8. This cake is heavy as (lead, led).
9. We had chocolate pudding for (desert, dessert).
10. Gina (choose, chose) a rocket ship for her birthday present.
11. Try not to (loose, lose) your head.
12. A sentry must not (desert, dessert) his post.
13. May I (advise, advice) you?
14. The time to speak of such matters is (passed, past).

Underline the word in parentheses that correctly completes each sentence.

15. The word *lose* rhymes with (kangaroos, rose).
16. The word *advise* rhymes with (ice, eyes).
17. The word *chose* rhymes with (twos, toes).
18. The word *whose* rhymes with (loose, lose).
19. The word *prize* rhymes with (advise, advice).
20. The word *rice* rhymes with (advise, advice).
21. The word *foes* rhymes with (choose, chose).
22 The word *noose* rhymes with (loose, lose).
23. The word *loose* rhymes with (moose, moos).
24. The word *advice* rhymes with (nice, size).
25. The word *choose* rhymes with (loose, lose).

22 Homophones and Apostrophes

A number of pronouns have forms that are homophones. Usually, one form is a possessive—for example, *your*—while the other is a contraction with a form of the verb *be*—you're. And usually, one form has an apostrophe, while the other does not.

The pairs are easy to distinguish if you remember these two rules:

1. Possessive forms of pronouns do *not* contain an apostrophe.
2. Contractions *do* contain an apostrophe.

Here are some homophones of this type. Study them carefully, making sure you understand where any apostrophe is placed.

its	Possessive of *it*.
it's	Contraction of *it is*.
your	Possessive of *you*.
you're	Contraction of *you are*.
whose	Possessive of *who*.
who's	Contraction of *who is*.

their	Possessive of *they*.
they're	Contraction of *they are*.
there	In that place (adverb). Also used in the expressions *there is* and *there are*.
theirs	Form of *their* used after a verb or the preposition *of*.
there's	Contraction of *there is*.

EXERCISES

In each sentence, underline the word in parentheses that best fits the meaning of the sentence.

1. We saw (your, you're) mother a minute ago.
2. (Whose, Who's) snake is this?
3. (Their, They're, There) once was a dragon named Herman.
4. (Its, It's) a lovely day today.
5. The mistake is (theirs, there's), not mine.
6. I want to know (whose, who's) responsible for this outrage.
7. We won't harm a hair of (their, they're, there) heads.
8. Don't go (their, they're, there).
9. I think (your, you're) out of your mind.
10. We think (their, they're, there) about to attack.
11. (Theirs, There's) something funny going on here.
12. (Its, It's) horrid little pink eyes glared at us.

Each of the following sentences contains a blank space that can be filled with some form of the word *they* or *there*. Write the form that belongs in each blank.

13. _____ all going to school.
14. _____ were two other choices we could have made.
15. Are you a friend of _____?
16. _____ a hair in my soup.
17. _____ tunnels were very oddly constructed.
18. Don't go _____ .

ANSWERS

1. your	7. their	13. They're
2. Whose	8. there	14. There
3. There	9. you're	15. theirs
4. It's	10. they're	16. There's
5. theirs	11. there's	17. Their
6. who's	12. Its	18. there

23 Homophones of Phrases and Numbers

There are two phrases that are homophones of single words. Study them carefully.

all ready	Totally ready.
already	By this time.
all together	All in the same place or all at the same time.
altogether	Completely.

Note one more frequently misspelled phrase:

all right	OK. (The spelling *alright* is incorrect.)

Here are some homophones involving the spelling of numbers:

two	2.
to	A preposition, or a word that can go in front of the root form of a verb.
too	Also.
four	4.
for	A preposition.
fourth	The one that stands in position number 4.
forth	Forward, or out of something.

Note another frequently misspelled word:

forty   40. (The spelling *fourty* is incorrect.)

EXERCISES

In each of the following sentences, underline the word in parentheses that best fits the meaning of the sentence.

1. What did you do that (four, for)?
2. This is the (fourth, forth) time I've had to speak to you.
3. I have forgotten it (all ready, already).
4. She forgot it (all together, altogether).
5. I waited two hours; then (fourty, forty) buses arrived at once.
6. I want (two, to, too) be a monster when I grow up.
7. Your car is (all ready, already), sir.
8. Jill heard the sound; I heard it (two, to, too).
9. We saw (two, to, too) hawks in the sky.
10. (All together, Altogether) now, pull!
11. Let's go (two, to, too) bed.
12. One of the guards came (fourth, forth) with a strange tale.
13. Everything looks (all right, alright).

ANSWERS

1. for
2. fourth
3. already
4. altogether
5. forty
6. to
7. all ready
8. too
9. two
10. All together
11. to
12. forth
13. all right

24 Review of Homophones

There is a no rule that can tell you how to choose between two homophones; you simply have to learn them. There are many others besides the ones in this book. The ones you have worked with are some of the most frequently confused.

Following is a list of the homophones in this book. See if you know the meaning of each one. If you are unsure, go back and check before you answer the review question on the next page.

Pages 48-49
brake, break
stake, steak
steel, steal
week, weak
plain, plane
waste, waist
real, reel
die, dye
right, write
whole, hole

Pages 50-51
affect, effect
accept, except
capital, capitol
miner, minor
principal, principle
stationary, stationery

Pages 52-53
formerly, formally
quite, quiet, quit
whether, weather
than, then
clothes, close, cloths
poor, pour, pore

Pages 54-55
choose, chose
loose, lose
advise, advice
lead, led
passed, past
desert, dessert

Pages 56-57
its, it's
your, you're
whose, who's
their, they're, there
theirs, there's

Pages 58-59
all ready, already
all together, altogether
all right
two, to, too
four, for
fourth, forth
forty

EXERCISES

The sentences below contain some of the homophones listed in this section. In each sentence, choose the word in parentheses that best fits the meaning of the sentence and underline it.

1. Don't (loose, lose) your keys.
2. This string is too (week, weak).
3. Nancy wrote her letters on purple (stationary, stationery).
4. He was a rather (quite, quiet, quit) child.
5. It is (all ready, already) night.
6. (Their, They're, There) about to begin.
7. Haste makes (waste, waist).
8. I'd like to know (whose, who's) idea this is.
9. Yesterday Elvin (lead, led) the class in singing folksongs.
10. The queen tried to (accept, except) the gift with a smile.
11. She (died, dyed) her skirt red.
12. Mommy, I don't have anything (two, to, too) do.
13. Will you (advise, advice) me on what to do?
14. That's the (whole, hole) truth, officer.
15. Are you sure (your, you're) feeling well?
16. Yes, I'm feeling (alright, all right).
17. (It's, Its) raining.
18. You can do whatever you (choose, chose).
19. I think we (passed, past) the turn ten minutes ago.
20. The governor walked up the (capital, capitol) steps.
21. We went about (fourty, forty) miles an hour.
22. The (principal, principle) thing to remember is to keep your powder dry.
23. Do you know (weather, whether) Countess Dracula will be here?
24. Does this have an (affect, effect) on you?
25. I hate to bother you with such a (miner, minor) matter.

ANSWERS

1. lose
2. weak
3. stationery
4. quiet
5. already
6. They're
7. waste
8. whose
9. led
10. accept
11. dyed
12. to
13. advise
14. whole
15. you're
16. all right
17. It's
18. choose
19. passed
20. capitol
21. forty
22. principal
23. whether
24. effect
25. minor

E

APOSTROPHES

This section deals with spelling problems involving words that contain an **apostrophe:** possessives like *Bill's* or *the dog's* and contractions like *isn't*, *you're*, and *let's*. You will study the general rules of how and when to use the apostrophe. You will also review certain pairs of words like *their* and *they're*, that are frequently confused.

25 Singular Possessives

The possessive of a noun in the singular is usually formed by adding an apostrophe plus –s:

> *a dog's tail*   *Mrs. Smith's house*
> *Bill's hat*   *the eagle's nest*

Words ending in *s* and containing only one syllable follow this general rule. They add the apostrophe plus –s:

> *my boss*   *my boss's opinion*
> *Miss Jones*   *Miss Jones's car*

Sometimes an apostrophe alone may be added. This may occur when a word contains more than one syllable and already ends in *s* or an *s* sound:

> *in Jesus' name*   *for goodness' sake*

Some people add an apostrophe alone to form the possessive of any noun ending in *s*. But this way of spelling a possessive does not reflect the average person's pronunciation. Try saying the possessive of *Jones* followed by the word *car*. Chances are that you say "*Joneses car*," not "*Jones car*." If you do, spell the possessive *Jones's*. If you do not, spell it *Jones'*. Let your spelling reflect your pronunciation.

Thus, the possessive of a word like *Hercules* could be spelled in either of two ways:

> *Hercules' club*   *Hercules's club*

The spelling you choose depends on how you would say the word.

EXERCISES

Write the possessive form of the word in parentheses in each sentence below. Let your spelling reflect your pronunciation.

 1. My (uncle) stories are hard to believe. _____
 2. The (horse) legs were covered with mud. _____
 3. The (picture) eyes followed me about the room. _____
 4. No one believed the (witness) story. _____
 5. (Alice) version was even stranger. _____
 6. Look at that (book) cover. _____
 7. It was (Morris) eighth year in the third grade. _____
 8. We were not convinced by (Doris) apologies. _____
 9. The (UN) flag is blue. _____
10. The townsmen were horrified by (Socrates) teaching.
    _____

ANSWERS

1. uncle's
2. horse's
3. picture's
4. witness's
5. Alice's

6. book's
7. Morris's ⎱ (Most people would say these
8. Doris's ⎰ possessives this way)
9. UN's
10. Socrates's or Socrates'

26 Plural Possessives

Nearly all plural possessives are formed by simply adding an apostrophe alone to the plural:

the horses' hoofs   *my parents' demands*

The few nouns with irregular plurals—that is, with plurals that do not end in *s*—add an apostrophe plus *–s:*

men's clothing   *the mice's tracks*

Follow these rules even with people's names:

the Joneses' house   *the Barrows' car*

When you spell the plural possessive of a singular noun, remember to form the plural first, then add the apostrophe:

horse   horses   horses'

EXERCISES

Write the possessive form of the following plural nouns:

1. roofs_____
2. children_____
3. women_____
4. Smiths_____
5. boxes_____

The following nouns are all in the singular. Write the plural possessive of each one. Remember—first form the plural, then the possessive.

6. tiger_____
7. craftsman_____
8. sailor_____
9. typist_____
10. fox_____

For each of the following nouns, write the singular possessive and the plural possessive.

11. box_____
12. house_____
13. foot_____
14. Peterson_____
15. student_____

ANSWERS

1. roofs'
2. children's
3. women's
4. Smiths'
5. boxes'
6. tigers'
7. craftsmen's
8. sailors'
9. typists'
10. foxes'
11. box's, boxes'
12. house's, houses'
13. foot's, feet's
14. Peterson's, Petersons'
15. student's, students'

27 Possessives of Pronouns

Personal pronouns—words like *I, you, he, she, it, we, they*—may have two possessive forms. For example, the possessive of *she* is either *her* or *hers*. The only possessives with but one form are *his* and *its*.

One of these possessive forms is used before a noun:

her book   *your* house   *our* friend

The other form is used whenever the possessive does not come before a noun—for example, when it occurs after a verb or the preposition *of*:

The book is *hers*.   The house is *yours*.   A friend of *ours*.

Notice two things about possessive pronouns. Many end in *s*. And they do *not* contain an apostrophe.

DO NOT USE AN APOSTROPHE TO FORM THE POSSESSIVE OF A PERSONAL PRONOUN!

Following this rule, the possessive of *it* is *its*, not *it's*. (The word *it's* is a contraction of *it is*, not a possessive.)

And the possessive of *who* is *whose*. Once again, no apostrophe.

You should, however, use the apostrophe to spell the possessive of words like *anyone* or *somebody* (*anyone's, somebody's*). These are **indefinite pronouns**, not personal pronouns, and they do not follow the rule for personal pronouns.

EXERCISES

Copy the italicized word in each of the following phrases or sentences. Add an apostrophe if necessary. If the word does not require an apostrophe, copy it without change.

1. *anybodys* guess _____
2. *its* eyes _____
3. an idea of *ours* _____
4. *Whose* book is this? _____
5. *someones* mistake _____
6. This rhinoceros must be *theirs*. _____

Write the correct possessive form of the pronoun in parentheses in each of the following sentences.

7. We all knew (who) car it was. _____
8. Is this toothbrush his or (she)? _____
9. The auto was a wreck; (it) side was completely caved in. _____
10. (Everybody) coat is in the closet. _____
11. I'm worried about this friend of (they). _____
12. I brought my half; did you remember (you)? _____

28 Contraction with NOT

You have just been working with the use of apostrophes in possessives. The second use of the apostrophe is to indicate a missing letter in a contraction.

A **contraction** is a running-together of two words (one of them a verb or an auxiliary) to form a single word. One of the most common kinds involves the contraction of the word *not* with one of the words that can be used in an auxiliary verb phrase, or with *do*. In this type of contraction, an apostrophe replaces the *o* of *not*:

> *is + not = isn't* *would + not = wouldn't*
> *have + not = haven't* *must + not = mustn't*

To write contractions like these, simply join the two words together and place an apostrophe to indicate the missing *o* in *not*.

Note the following three irregularly formed contractions:

> *can + not = can't* *shall + not = shan't* *will + not = won't*

The spelling of the verb changes, but the apostrophe still replaces the *o* in *not*.

You should avoid one possible mistake: putting the apostrophe in the wrong place. Spellings like *do'nt* and *was'nt* are incorrect. Remember, the apostrophe is used to indicate a missing letter.

EXERCISES

Copy the italicized word in each of the following sentences, adding an apostrophe in the proper place.

1. We *werent* sure which road to take._____
2. *Dont* you even know in what year Columbus discovered America?

   _____
3. The teacher *couldnt* convince Frederick that the earth goes around the sun._____
4. Mommy, Billy *wont* let me play with his toy train._____
5. I *shant* be long._____

Write the contraction in the blank space after each pair of words.

6. can + not_____
7. will + not_____
8. shall + not_____
9. might + not_____
10. would + not_____
11. must + not_____
12. does + not_____

ANSWERS

1. weren't
2. Don't
3. couldn't
4. won't
5. shan't
6. can't
7. won't
8. shan't
9. mightn't
10. wouldn't
11. mustn't
12. doesn't

29 Other Contractions with Verbs

Whether used as main verbs or as auxiliaries, the verbs *be* and *have* and the "helping" verbs *will* and *would* form certain standard contractions with pronouns and nouns. As usual, the apostrophe takes the place of a missing letter or letters. Here are some examples, using pronouns:

I + am = I'm	*you + will = you'll*	*I + had = I'd*
you + are = you're	*I + have = I've*	*I + would = I'd*
it + is = it's	*it + has = it's*	*who + is = who's*

Here are a few things to remember about contractions like these:

1. Nouns can form contractions: *Carla's not at home* is a contracted form of *Carla is not at home.*

2. Contractions with *is* have the same form as contractions with *has*: the contraction *he's* can be either *he is* or *he has.* Your basic understanding of English will tell you which of the two is meant in a given context.

3. Contractions with *had* have the same form as contractions with *would*: the contraction *he'd* can be either *he had* or *he would.*

4. No matter how many letters are dropped in the contraction, you need only one apostrophe to replace them.

5. *It's* is a contraction. *Its* is a possessive.

6. Other common contractions with *is* are *there's, where's* and *what's.*

7. A final contraction you should know is *let's* (*let us*).

EXERCISES

Copy the italicized word in each of the following sentences, adding an apostrophe in the proper place.

1. *Theres* something strange going on here._____
2. *Youve* got something crawling up your back._____
3. *Ill* try to get it for you. _____
4. *Hes* going to the movies tonight._____
5. *Whos* making all that noise?_____
6. *Bloods* thicker than water._____
7. *Anns* a rather strange girl._____

Write the contractions indicated below:

8. I + have_____
9. he + has_____
10. she + is_____
11. you + would_____
12. Barry + is_____
13. what + is_____
14. they + are_____
15. we + had_____

ANSWERS

1. There's	8. I've
2. You've	9. he's
3. I'll	10. she's
4. He's	11. you'd
5. Who's	12. Barry's
6. Blood's	13. what's
7. Ann's	14. they're
	15. we'd

30 Common Confusions with Apostrophes

You may have noticed that several possessive pronouns are pronounced like contractions—for example, *its* and *it's*, or *whose* and *who's*. These similarly pronounced words are often confused in writing. To help you keep them straight, here is a listing of the most commonly confused forms:

its	*it's*	
whose	*who's*	
your	*you're*	
their	*they're*	*there*
theirs	*there's*	

The words in the first column are possessive pronouns. Remember, none contains an apostrophe.

The words in the second column are all contractions with *is* or *are*. An apostrophe replaces the missing letter or letters.

The word *there* in the third column is often confused with two forms of the pronoun *they*: the possessive *their* and the contraction *they're*. Be careful of this possible confusion. Similarly, *there's*, the contraction of *there + is*, is often confused with the possessive *theirs*.

74

EXERCISES

In each of the following sentences, underline the word in parentheses that fits the meaning of the sentence.

1. We wanted to know (whose, who's) idea it was._____
2. Are (their, they're, there) bags packed yet?_____
3. (Its, It's) raining outside._____
4. (Their, They're, There) are two big highways that lead out of town.
   _____
5. (Your, You're) looking well._____
6. (Your, You're) clothes are wet._____
7. I'm a friend of (theirs, there's)._____
8. (Who's, Whose) in charge here?_____
9. You can't tell a book by (its, it's) cover._____
10. (Theirs, There's) Admiral Grommet, singing old songs of the sea in his cracked voice._____
11. (Their, They're, There) coming to dinner tonight._____

Look carefully at the italicized word in each of the following sentences. In some sentences, it is correct. In other sentences, it is misspelled, or the wrong form is used. Write the correct form for each example. (If the word is already correct, all you will have to do is copy it.)

12. Who goes *their*?_____
13. *It's* not easy._____
14. I wonder *whose* next._____
15. Never pick up a rattlesnake by *it's* tail._____
16. Those kids of *their's* give me a pain._____
17. *There* all waiting at the beach._____
18. *Theres* nothing to be done about it._____
19. *Your* plane is about to leave._____
20. Make sure *your* on time._____

ANSWERS

1. whose
2. their
3. It's
4. There
5. You're
6. Your

7. theirs
8. Who's
9. its
10. There's
11. They're
12. there
13. It's

14. who's
15. its
16. theirs
17. They're
18. There's
19. Your
20. you're

31 Review of Apostrophes

Here is a review of the main uses of the apostrophe discussed in this book.

POSSESSIVES

1. Add an apostrophe plus –s to form the possessive of a noun in the singular: *cat's, Bill's, Grace's.*

2. If a noun in the singular ends in s and has more than one syllable, you may choose to form its possessive with an apostrophe alone if you pronounce it that way. Common examples are *Jesus', goodness'.*

3. Add an apostrophe alone to form the possessive of a noun in the plural that ends in s: *dogs', Joneses'.*

4. Add an apostrophe plus –s to form the possessive of plural nouns that do *not* end in s: *men's, women's.*

5. The possessive form of a personal pronoun does not contain an apostrophe: *its, theirs, yours, whose.*

6. The possessive form of an indefinite pronoun ends in an apostrophe plus –s: *anyone's, somebody's.*

CONTRACTIONS

1. An apostrophe replaces the missing letter or letters in a contraction: *isn't, I'm, let's.*

2. Common contractions include: *be, have, do,* and helping verbs with *not*; and nouns and pronouns with *be, have, will,* and *would.*

3. Commonly confused words involving apostrophes are *its* and *it's; your* and *you're; whose* and *who's; there, their,* and *they're;* and *theirs* and *there's.*

EXERCISES

Write the possessive of each of the following words:

1. he_____
2. who_____
3. Nathan_____
4. Bess_____
5. anybody_____

Write the plural possessives of each of the following words:

6. child_____
7. doctor_____
8. Hess (a person's last name)

_____

9. mouse_____
10. house_____

Write the contractions indicated below:

11. is + not_____
12. he + is_____
13. he + has_____
14. will + not_____
15. shall + not_____

In each of the following sentences, underline the word in parentheses that fits the meaning of the sentence.

16. I think (theirs, there's) a better way.
17. Do you know (its, it's) name?
18. Bill thinks that (your, you're) his friend.
19. I'm sure (their, there, they're) on the way.

ANSWERS

1. his
2. whose
3. Nathan's
4. Bess's
5. anybody's
6. children's
7. doctors'
8. Hesses'
9. mice's
10. houses'
11. isn't
12. he's
13. he's
14. won't
15. shan't
16. there's
17. its
18. you're
19. they're

F

CAPITALIZATION

This section will introduce you to certain types of words that are usually spelled with a capital letter. Most such words are called **proper nouns**—words like *Nancy*, or *Texas*, or *Christmas*. This section will show you how to identify nouns of this type. In addition, it will discuss other types of words that are customarily capitalized, such as adjectives formed from proper nouns, and words in book titles.

32 Capitalizing Names and Titles

The general rule for capitalizing words is easy to understand. Capitalize proper nouns; do not capitalize a common noun unless it is the first word in a sentence.

A **proper noun** is the name of a particular or unique person, place, or thing. A **common noun** is a general name that can be applied to any number of persons or things. For examples of the difference, look at these two sentences:

> The *man* lives on a *street* near a *hill.*
> *Randolph* lives on *Broad Street* near *Bald Hill.*

Words like *man*, *street*, and *hill* in the first sentence are common nouns. In the second sentence, they have been replaced by proper nouns: *Randolph, Broad Street,* and *Bald Hill*—the names of a particular man, street, and hill.

People's names, initials, and nicknames are capitalized:

Dee Sanchez	*Lefty*	*Sitting Bull*
Big Bill	*P. T. Barnum*	*Napoleon*

Titles before a person's name are also capitalized:

Mrs. Harris	*Rear Admiral* Sudd	*Queen Victoria*
Dr. Obispo	*Uncle* Mort	*Judge* Crater

When a title alone is used as a noun of address—that is, when someone is being spoken to by his title--the title is capitalized:

> Good morning, *Doctor.*
> I object, *Your Honor.*

If the title is one of great honor, nobility, or high office, it is capitalized when it is used in place of the person's name:

The President will see you now.
The Secretary of State coughed gently.

Lesser titles are not usually capitalized unless they precede a person's name or are used as nouns of address:

The *doctor* will see you now.
My *uncle* is a very strange man.
The *treasurer* of our club cannot add very well.

Finally, names of relatives like *mother* and *father* are usually capitalized when they are used in place of a name. They are not usually capitalized when preceded by a modifying word like *the, my,* or *his:*

My *mother* asked *Grandfather* to visit us for a week.
We gave *Dad* a kite for his birthday.

EXERCISES

Write the words from each of the following sentences that should be spelled with capitals. You may omit the first word of each sentence, which is already capitalized. Be careful—there may be several words in each sentence that you should capitalize. Be sure to use capitals when you write your answers.

1. Howls of rage echoed through the castle when duke otto read the letter._____
2. My aunt seemed to think that mother was not strict enough with henry. _____
3. The sailors had contempt for admiral grommet's seamanship, but they respected his temper. _____
4. Every evening mr. soames read a few of the sayings of confucius.

   _____
5. I'm afraid dad will throttle me when he finishes talking with the teacher._____
6. Tell me, senator, how do you intend to vote on the president's new bill? _____
7. I wouldn't vote for emory q. fairfax for dogcatcher.

   _____
8. Excuse me, officer, but is this the way to the beach?

   _____
9. Stand up for the king! _____
10. Always address the ambassador as your excellency.

    _____

ANSWERS

1. Duke Otto
2. Mother, Henry
3. Admiral Grommet
4. Mr. Soames, Confucius
5. Dad
6. Senator, President's
7. Emory Q. Fairfax
8. Officer
9. King
10. Ambassador (if you wish to show respect), Your Excellency

Capitalizing Place Names

Names of particular places are considered proper nouns and should be capitalized. For example:

Mount Everest   *Lake Erie*   *Roman Empire*
England   *Bryant Park*   *Hudson River*
New York State   *Golden Gate Bridge*   *Chicago*
Pacific Ocean   *Orange County*   *Mojave Desert*

Notice that words like *state, ocean, lake, park* and *empire* are capitalized only when they are part of the name. They would not be capitalized in sentences like these:

The Pacific is the largest *ocean* in the world.
The *state* of New York contains over 10 million people.
The *delta* of the Mississippi extends out from Louisiana.

Do not capitalize little words like *the* or *of,* even when they are part of a place name:

the Bay *of* Fundy
the Gulf *of* California

Do not capitalize directions like *east* or *west* unless you are writing about a region of the country:

Birds fly *south* for the winter.
BUT: Alabama is part of the *South.*

EXERCISES

Write all the words from the following sentences that should be capitalized. Be sure to use capitals when you write them.

1. The street names in the state of hawaii are hard for newcomers to pronounce._____
2. One street is named kalanianaole highway; another is kalakaua avenue._____
3. Fortunately, the main street of honolulu is called king street.
   _____
4. Cowboys used to drive cattle across the plains of the west.
   _____
5. Sandor traveled to lake titicaca, high in the andes mountains of peru._____

Some of the following sentences contain personal names and titles as well as place names. Once again, write the words that should be spelled with capitals.

6. I tell you, general, the public will never elect mr. lincoln as president of the united states._____
   _____
7. The ruler of the little country of hunza, high in the himalaya mountains, is called the mir._____
   _____
8. The great basin is a region of the u.s. that lies between the rockies and the sierra nevada of california._____
   _____
9. In the last century a man named james brooke set himself up as ruler of a part of the island of borneo._____
   _____
10. The mountains in alaska are the highest in the continent of north america._____

ANSWERS

1. Hawaii
2. Kalanianaole Highway, Kalakaua Avenue
3. Honolulu, King Street
4. West (You can capitalize Plains if you think of it as a distinct region.)
5. Sandor, Lake Titicaca, Andes Mountains, Peru
6. General, Mr. Lincoln, President, United States
7. Hunza, Himalaya Mountains (Mir might also be capitalized.)
8. Great Basin, U.S., Rockies, Sierra Nevada, California
9. James Brooke, Borneo
10. Alaska, North America

34 Capitalizing Names of Organizations

The names of individual organizations are capitalized.

Churches and names of religions:

Protestant Church   *Buddhism*
Christianity   *Church of Christ*

Government organizations:

Congress   *U.S. Army*
Senate   *Department of Justice*

Names of schools, companies, etc.:

Grant Park High School   *Federal Deposit Insurance*
University of Wisconsin   *Corporation*
Red Cross   *Associated Press*
General Motors

Do not capitalize words like *church, army, department, high school,* or *corporation* unless they are part of the name of a particular organization.

And do not capitalize little words like *a, the, of,* or *and* unless they begin a sentence.

EXERCISES

Underline the words in each of the following sentences that should be capitalized.

1. I opened a bank account at the first national trust company.

2. Then I found out that the bank's president was wanted by the federal bureau of investigation.

3. The department of the army is part of the defense department.

4. A strange gentleman asked mr. lewis to contribute to the chastek paralysis society.

5. The national religion of india is hinduism.

6. Our high school was thoroughly trounced in basketball by general grant high school.

7. Among the national organizations that issue credit cards are diners club and american express.

8. The dinosaur skeleton in the museum of natural history is almost thirty feet tall.

9. The standard oil company of rhode island is one of the smallest companies in the world.

10. The bells in st. basil's church are completely out of tune.

ANSWERS

1. First National Trust Company
2. Federal Bureau (of) Investigation (Don't capitalize *of*!)
3. Department (of the) Army, Defense Department
4. Mr. Lewis, Chastek Paralysis Society
5. India, Hinduism
6. General Grant High School
7. Diners Club, American Express
8. Museum (of) Natural History
9. Standard Oil Company (of) Rhode Island
10. Saint Basil's Church

Capitalizing Proper Adjectives and Similar Words

Certain adjectives are formed from or related to proper nouns. For example, the adjective *French* comes from the proper noun *France*. Adjectives formed from or related to proper nouns are called **proper adjectives**, and they are capitalized just like the proper nouns to which they are related.

> *French* wines
> an *Irish* wolfhound
> a *South American* journey

Notice that the nouns modified by a proper adjective are not necessarily capitalized.

Related to proper adjectives are certain types of words often used to identify someone as a member of a particular group. Take, for example, an imaginary man named Mr. Badhand who may be described as follows:

nationality:	*American*
ethnic group:	*Indian (or Native American)*
tribe:	*Dakota Sioux*
language he speaks:	*English and Dakota*
religion:	*Roman Catholic*
his political party:	*Democratic*
residence:	*South Dakotan*

Whether used as adjectives or as nouns, words like the ones that describe Mr. Badhand are capitalized. (Exceptions: words like *white* or *black*, referring to races, are usually not capitalized.)

EXERCISES

Copy and capitalize each word in the following sentences that should be written with a capital letter.

1. The indian elephant is a more easily trained beast than the african elephant._____

2. The nest of the baltimore oriole usually hangs down beneath the branch of a tree._____

3. The doctor says I have asian flu._____

4. Many mohawk indians are steelworkers._____
_____

5. Spluttering wildly in german, duke otto backed away from his resolute foe._____

6. Her favorite foods were mexican tamales, maine lobster, and mississippi river catfish._____
_____

7. Sandor decided to visit several south american countries._____
_____

8. This news caused quite a stir in several european capitals._____
_____

9. Large numbers of swiss, danish, and belgian merchants had become very rich selling souvenirs to him._____
_____

10. Now they faced losing their best american customer to the brazilians._____

1. Indian, African
2. Baltimore
3. Asian
4. Mohawk Indians
5. German, Duke Otto
6. Mexican, Maine, Mississippi River
7. South American
8. European
9. Swiss, Danish, Belgian
10. American, Brazilians

36 Other Words Spelled with Capitals

Below are a few other kinds of words that you should spell with capitals:

Days of the week and names of months—but not seasons:

Sunday   *February*   *autumn*
Monday   *March*   *winter*

Holidays:

Christmas   *Lincoln's Birthday*
Independence Day   *Columbus Day*

Names of particular historical events, battles, wars, or ages:

Battle of the Bulge   *Space Age*
World War II   *Atomic Era*

Brand names—but not any words they modify:

Coca-Cola   *Ivory soap*
Kleenex   *Chevrolet station wagon*

EXERCISES

Underline the words in each of the following sentences that should be written with capitals.

1. Every saturday in spring and summer, a group of kite fliers meets in central park.
2. On new year's day mr. manship made ten resolutions.
3. By the end of january he had broken every one.
4. The teacher remarked that frederick's ideas of geography were straight out of the middle ages.
5. The battle of bull run was the first major battle of the civil war.
6. The autumn leaves look their best in october.
7. Mrs. winthrop's ford tractor broke down in the middle of spring plowing.
8. School opens on the tuesday after labor day.
9. Throughout the entire revolutionary war, general granger sat in his bedroom and sulked.
10. And that is why on february 22, we celebrate washington's birthday instead of the birthday of general granger.

37 Capitalizing Titles of Books, Stories, etc.

Most words in the titles of books, stories, plays, and poems are capitalized. (In addition, book titles are underlined or printed in italics, while titles of stories are set off with quotations marks.)

Here are the rules for capitalizing titles:

1. Always capitalize the first and last words of the title, no matter what they are.

2. Unless it is the first or last word of the title, do not capitalize

   the words *the, a;* or *an*
   short conjunctions like *and* or *or*
   short prepositions like *in, at, with,* or *to*

3. Capitalize all other words, including prepositions of more than four letters like *against, through,* or *before.*

Here are some examples:

What Men Live By
Two Years Before the Mast
Patterns of Survival
The Forging of Our Continent
In Wildness Is the Preservation of the World

EXERCISES

Copy the following titles, capitalizing them correctly.

1. birds of prey of the world

   _____

2. report from practically nowhere

   _____

3. on aggression

   _____

4. death and the supreme court

   _____

5. you can do it, charlie brown

   _____

6. the lord of the rings

   _____

7. great tales of terror and the supernatural

   _____

8. mary poppins opens the door

   _____

9. the bridge of san luis rey

   _____

10. my horses, my teachers

   _____

ANSWERS

1. *Birds of Prey of the World*
2. *Report from Practically Nowhere*
3. *On Aggression*
4. *Death and the Supreme Court*
5. *You Can Do It, Charlie Brown*
6. *The Lord of the Rings*
7. *Great Tales of Terror and the Supernatural*
8. *Mary Poppins Opens the Door*
9. *The Bridge of San Luis Rey*
10. *My Horses, My Teachers*

38 Review of Capitalization

Here is a review of the types of words that are customarily spelled with capitals.

Proper nouns, nicknames, and initials

All titles of respect when they precede the name, or when they are used as nouns of address

Titles of honor, nobility, or high office, when they are used in place of a person's name

Words showing relationship, when not preceded by words like *my* or *the*

Place names

Names of organizations, political bodies, religions, etc.

Proper adjectives

Days of the week, names of months, and holidays

Names of historical events, periods, wars, and battles

Brand names

The first and last words of the title of a book, story, poem, or play, plus other words in the title except short prepositions, conjunctions, and words like *or*, *an*, and *the*.

EXERCISES

Underline each word in the following sentences that should be written with a capital letter.

1. The secretary of defense listened gravely to doctor harper's report.

2. Although he was plainly in his early thirties, sergeant monroe was able to fool the tourists into believing he was the only living soldier to have fought at custer's last stand.

3. Every summer, from june to september, he would thrill thousands of visitors with his descriptions of the battle.

4. His information was totally inaccurate—for example, he placed the battle in eastern north dakota, about four hundred miles from the part of the state of montana where it actually occurred.

5. However, his habit of answering questions in the french canadian language was oddly convincing, and, more important, general custer was not around to contradict him.

6. At the climax of his performance, he peddled copies of his book, *the battle on the high plains*, at ten dollars a copy.

7. He had made enough money to buy three toyota station wagons—one for his father, one for his mother, and one for himself.

8. Finally the national park service in washington, d.c., put a stop to these activities.

9. Sergeant monroe is now richer than ever; he travels from california to new york giving lectures.

10. And at the end of each lecture, he sells autographed copies of his new book, *my fight against the bureaucrats in washington*, at twenty dollars a copy.

ANSWERS

1. Secretary (of) Defense, Doctor Harper's
2. Sergeant Monroe, Custer's Last Stand
3. June, September
4. North Dakota, Montana
5. French Canadian, General Custer
6. *The Battle* (*on the*) *High Plains*
7. Toyota
8. National Park Service, Washington, D.C.
9. (Sergeant) Monroe, California, New York
10. *My Fight Against* (*the*) *Bureaucrats* (*in*) *Washington*

G

SPELLING & THE DICTIONARY

One of the most useful sources of spelling information is a dictionary. This section will introduce you to some of the different kinds of spelling information that are contained in your dictionary and will give you practice in locating and using such information.

You will need to use a dictionary as you work through this section. In many of the exercises, you will be asked to use it to look up words. So be sure you have a dictionary on hand before you begin.

39 Spelling Information in the Main Entry

The main entry of a dictionary word shows you how to spell the word, of course. There are, in addition, certain special types of spelling information to watch for in the main entry:

1. Syllable Divisions. When a word contains more than one syllable, it is entered in the dictionary with a small space between each syllable. Many dictionaries insert a dot or a very short dash in the spaces. Here is how three different dictionaries might show the syllables of the word *exaggeration*:

ex ag ger a tion
ex•ag•ger•a•tion
ex–ag–ger–a–tion

In your writing, whenever you have to hyphenate a word at the conclusion of a line (as in the line above), the break should occur between syllables. Your dictionary will show you where the syllable breaks occur.

2. Hyphenation. Some words are always spelled with a hyphen. The dictionary entry will show this hyphen, if there is one. If your dictionary is one that uses small dashes to show syllable divisions, it will use a longer dash to show a hyphen: o–rang—u–tan.

3. Word Divisions. Some dictionary entries consist of two words. A two-word entry will usually have a large space between the two words. If your dictionary is one that uses a small space between syllables, be careful not to confuse this with the large space between words. For example:

corn cob (one word)
corn   bread (two words)

4. Capitalization. If a word is usually spelled with a capital, its entry will also be spelled with a capital. If a word has two uses but only one

of them is capitalized, the dictionary may list them under two entries—
for example, **God** (the Almighty) and **god** (any supernatural being that
is worshiped).

EXERCISES

Write your answers to the following questions. Refer to your dictionary
whenever necessary.

1. How does your own dictionary mark syllables? (Check A, B, or C)
    ☐ A. With a small space between syllables
    ☐ B. With a dot between syllables
    ☐ C. With a small dash between syllables

2. What is the first main entry in your dictionary to contain five syl-
    lables? (Start at the beginning of the A's and count the syllables of
    each entry until you find the first one with five.)

Place a check mark (✔) in the box before each of the following words that
is correctly divided into syllables. Place an X in the box before the number of each word that is *not* correctly divided into syllables.

☐ 3. ev•er
☐ 4. ev•ery
☐ 5. dom•in•ate
☐ 6. au•thor

Some of the following words are correctly spelled. Others contain a
spelling mistake. Look up each word in your dictionary. If it is
spelled correctly, place a check mark (✔) before its number. If it is
misspelled, copy it on the line after it with the correct spelling. Watch
for hyphens and word divisions.

7. muskox _____
8. muskrat _____
9. cornmeal _____
10. cornstarch _____
11. humming-bird _____
12. great grandmother _____

ANSWERS

1. Your answer depends on what dictionary you use.
2. In most dictionaries, *abbreviation*.
3. ✔
4. X
5. X
6. ✔
7. musk ox (most dictionaries: but yours may be different)
8. ✔
9. Some dictionaries spell this as two words, others as one word. Follow your own dictionary.
10. ✔
11. hummingbird
12. great-grandmother

40 Spelling Information Outside the Main Entry

Sometimes a dictionary can provide help in spelling certain kinds of words that may not be listed as main entries. These are special grammatical forms or suffixed forms. Here are some:

1. **Comparative** and **Superlative** Forms of Adjectives. For example, the two words *crazier* and *craziest*, which are formed from *crazy*.
2. Verb Forms. For example, the words *crackled* and *crackling*, which are formed from the verb *crackle*.
3. Suffixed Forms. For example, the adverb *craftily* and the noun *craftiness*, which are formed from the adjective *crafty*.
4. Noun Plurals. For example, the word *babies*, which is formed from *baby*.

The above example words are *not* always main entry words, although the words from which they are formed *are* main entries. They are often listed within the entry of the word from which they are formed. Sometimes they are near the beginning of the entry, sometimes at the end—it depends on which dictionary you are using. **You can spot them easily, however, because they are printed in heavy black letters to make them stand out.**

Not all possible grammatical or suffixed forms are listed after the main entry. Those that are listed are often those that involve spelling problems. There is no listing for the word *dogs*, for instance, since spelling this plural merely involves adding *-s* to *dog*. But when you form the plural of *baby*, you change the *y* to an *i* and add *-es*. This presents a spelling problem to those who don't know the spelling rule for the plural of this noun, so *babies* is listed in the *baby* entry.

EXERCISES

Write the form indicated in each of the following exercises *without* looking it up in your dictionary. When you have completed all 10, look up each one in your dictionary. Cross out any error you made and write the correct form in its place. (Hints: your dictionary may list some of these as main entries. If you cannot find a form after a careful search, it is probably formed in a regular way, by adding a suffix without a spelling change.)

1. The plural of *silo*. _____
2. The plural of *tornado*. _____
3. The plural of *hobby*. _____
4. The present participle (the form that ends in *-ing*) of *marry*.
   _____
5. The present participle of *employ*. _____
6. The past tense of *marry*. _____
7. The past tense of *employ*. _____
8. The superlative (the form ending in *-est*) of *silly*.
   _____
9. The comparative (the form ending in *-er*) of *gay*.
   _____
10. The adverb (with an *-ly* ending) formed from *noble*.
    _____

ANSWERS

1. silos
2. tornadoes or tornados
3. hobbies
4. marrying
5. employing

6. married
7. employed
8. silliest
9. gayer
10. nobly

41 Variant Spellings

As you are undoubtedly aware, many words have more than one spelling. You have already encountered one such word—the plural of *tornado*—in the last set of exercises.

When a word has two common spellings, the dictionary will often include them both. Different dictionaries will list them in different ways, however. Here are some of the main ways they may be listed:

1. The most common spelling will be a main entry, with a full definition after it.

2. Alternate, less common spellings are sometimes listed in the body of the main entry, either near the beginning or at the end. These other spellings may be preceded by the word *or* or *also*. They are usually printed in heavy black type, so they are easy to pick out.

3. The less common spelling may also have an entry of its own. It will not have a full definition after it, however. It will usually be followed only by the more common, or "preferred" spelling. For example:

sul•phur (sul′fər)   n. sulfur.

If you are in doubt about which of two variant spellings to use in your own writing, use the one with the full definition after it. It is usually the most common spelling.

EXERCISES

Each of the following words has a variant spelling. Find each variant in your dictionary and write it after the word it goes with.

1. judgement _____
2. fledgeling _____
3. sulphur _____
4. margarin _____
5. orang-outang _____
6. cantaloup _____
7. adz _____
8. axe _____
9. carousel _____
10. inclose _____

Below are some pairs of variant spellings. Write the spelling you should use in your own writing. (Use your dictionary to choose the more common, or preferred form.)

11. theater, theatre _____
12. center, centre _____
13. honor, honour _____
14. broncho, bronco _____
15. chanty, chantey _____

ANSWERS

1. judgment
2. fledgling
3. sulfur
4. margarine
5. orang-utan
6. cantaloupe
7. adze
8. ax

9. carrousel
10. enclose
11. theater ⎫
12. center ⎪
13. honor ⎬ Most dictionaries consider these the most common spellings in American English.
14. bronco ⎪
15. chantey ⎭

 # Spelling of Sounds at the Beginning of Words

Before you look up a word in a dictionary, you must have some idea how to spell it. This is sometimes difficult, because the same sound may be spelled in many different ways.

Below is a simplified table of some of the common alternate ways that sounds can be spelled at the beginning of words. When you look up a word that begins with any of these sounds and cannot find it where you expect to, try looking under one of the letters in the table. For example, if you didn't know how to spell the word *coin*, you would probably look first under the letter *k*. You wouldn't find it there, of course. But if you then looked under the letter *c*, as indicated in the table, you would find it.

CONSONANT SOUNDS	COMMON ALTERNATE SPELLINGS	CONSONANT SOUNDS	COMMON ALTERNATE SPELLINGS
b, d, l, m, p, sh, t, th, v, and *w*	Usually spelled the way they sound	*n* as in nice	*kn* (know), *gn* (gnaw), *pn* (pneumonia)
f as in face	*ph* (phone)	*r* as in rice	*rh* (rhino), *wr* (write)
g as in gas	*gh* (ghost), *gu* (guard)	*s* as in save	*c* followed by *e, i,* or *y* (cent), *sce* (scent), *sci* (science)
h as in hole	*wh* (who)		
j as in join	*g* followed by *e, i,* or *y:* (gentle, gin, gym)	*sk* as in skin	*sc* (score), *sch* (school)
k as in kitten	*c* (coin), *ch* (chord), *qu* (queer)	*z* as in zone	*x* (xylophone)
		ch as in child	*c* (cello)

VOWEL SOUNDS	COMMON ALTERNATE SPELLINGS	VOWEL SOUNDS	COMMON ALTERNATE SPELLINGS
ā as in able	ai (aim)	ō as in open	oa (oats), ow (owe)
ă as in at	a (at)	ŏ as in hot	o (odd), (see also a as in father)
ã as in area	ai (air), e (ere)	ô as in often	aw (awful), oa (oar), a (all), au (auto), ou (ought)
ä as in father	a (argument)		
ē as in equal	ea (eat), ee (eel), ei (either)	ou as in out	ow (owl)
ĕ as in lend	e (end)	ū as in use	you (youth), eu (eulogy)
ėr as in her	er (ermine), ear (earth), ur (urge)	ŭ as in up	o (oven)
ī as in ice	ei (either)	ə —the unstressed vowel sound that begins about, event, oblige, upon	a, e, i, o, u
ĭ as in hit	i (it), e (electric)		

EXERCISES

In each of the following items, a misspelled word is followed by a definition. Try to guess the correct spelling, using the table you have just read as a guide, and check your spelling in the dictionary. When you find the correct spelling, write it on your paper. Two words have been done for you, as examples.

nock (to strike or hit)   Answer: knock
ider (*i* pronounced as in *ice*; a kind of duck)   Answer: eider

1. filter (a love potion or a magic drink) _____
2. goul (a monster that haunts graveyards) _____
3. rack (wreckage; ruin; also, a kind of seaweed) _____
4. zylem (part of the bark of a tree) _____
5. klorine (a greenish-yellow poison gas) _____
6. esel (*e* pronounced as in *equal*; a stand for a painting)

_____

7. erl (*er* pronounced as in *her*; a noble lord) _____
8. ucalyptus (*u* pronounced as in *use*; an Australian tree)

_____

9. oricle (*o* pronounced as in *often*; a part of the heart)

_____

10. irode (*i* pronounced as in *hit*; to wear away or eat away)

_____

ANSWERS

1. philter
2. ghoul
3. wrack
4. xylem
5. chlorine
6. easel
7. earl
8. eucalyptus
9. auricle
10. erode

43 The Dictionary Spelling Chart—Consonants

If you can spell the first three or four letters of a word, you can usually find the word in a dictionary. For example, if you know or guess that the word *tongue* begins with the letters *t-o-n,* you will have to check only a few words beginning with these letters to find *tongue.*

Most dictionaries contain a chart or table of possible spellings of sounds like the one you worked with on the last two pages. This table usually gives the possible spellings of sounds in any part of a word, not just the spellings at the beginning of words.

Open your dictionary to the sections at the beginning of the book, before the main entry listings, and find this table of the possible spellings of sounds. The table is usually called something like *Common Spellings of English,* or *Spelling Chart.* It may be a double chart like *Consonant Sounds* and *Vowel Sounds.* (In one dictionary it is included as part of the pronunciation guide.) You may have to look through several pages to find this table.

When you have found this table, take five or ten minutes to look over the spellings for the consonants. (You'll take up vowel spellings in the next section.) You will find that the table in your dictionary includes several spellings that were not included in the table you just worked with in this book. Most of these spellings that do not occur at the beginning of words—doubled consonants, for instance, like the *bb* in *bubble,* or combinations like the /f/ sound of *gh* in *rough.* (Throughout this section /   / means the sound of the letter inside the slash marks.)

EXERCISES

Following the same procedure as in the last set of exercises, write the correct spellings of the following misspelled words. Use the table in your dictionary as a guide, and look up each word in your dictionary to make sure you are spelling it correctly. (The misspellings are in the italicized portion of the words.)

1. fil*tch* (to steal)
2. fa*llk*on (kind of hawk)
3. fi*sh*on (splitting into two or more parts)
4. pre*sh*us (very valuable)
5. stri*ckcher* (a critical remark; a narrowing; a limitation)
6. ba*n*er (a flag)

ANSWERS

1. filch
2. falcon
3. fission

4. precious
5. stricture
6. banner

44 The Dictionary Spelling Chart—Vowels

If you look at the vowel spellings in the spelling chart in your dictionary, you will notice that vowel sounds have many more possible spellings than consonant sounds do. Here are a few hints that may help you as you look over the table.

The schwa sound (ə: the unstressed vowel sound found in the first syllable of *alone* and *upon*, and in the last syllable of *places* and *circus*) can be spelled by any vowel. Usually, only one vowel is used, except in the letter combinations *ous* and *ain* (*famous, mountain*).

Long vowels (the vowels marked with a (⁻) over them: $\bar{a}, \bar{e}, \bar{i}, \bar{o}, \bar{u}$) have the largest number of possible spellings. A word with a long vowel in the last syllable often has a final, "silent" *e* (*hope, made*). Long vowels are seldom found before doubled consonants. Many long vowel sounds are spelled with two-letter combinations: *ai* (aim), *ei* or *ie* (ceiling, piece), etc.

Short vowels (the vowels with no marks over them or with a ˘ over them: *a* or *ă*, etc.) are often found before doubled consonants (rabbit, winner). Short vowels are more often spelled the way they sound than long vowels are.

Watch for unusual combinations of letters like *ough*, which can be pronounced in different ways: *through, though, rough, ought*.

Now look over the vowel spellings in the spelling chart in your dictionary. Take a little more time to study them than you did the consonants. You will need more time, since there are more spellings.

EXERCISES

Write the correct spellings of the following misspelled words. Use the spelling chart in your dictionary as a guide, and look up each word to make sure you are spelling in correctly. (As before, the misspellings are in the italicized portions of the words.)

1. *ree*m (an amount of paper—480 to 516 sheets)——————————
2. *ai*ncient (old)——————————
3. *leeay*son (contacts between groups of an army)——————————
4. ha*w*nch (the hips, or loin, of an animal)——————————
5. *you* (a kind of evergreen tree)——————————
6. pr*ay* (any animal hunted for food; a victim)——————————

ANSWERS

1. ream
2. ancient
3. liaison
4. haunch
5. yew
6. prey

H
SUMMARY & REVIEW

This section will give you the opportunity to go over what you have learned about spelling skills. All the major rules and skills-building techniques taught in this book are summarized here, arrranged in the same order as the sections of the book. You can use this section to review what you have learned. You may wish to keep it permanently to refer to in the future.

45 Summary & Review: Prefixes & Suffixes

When a <u>prefix</u> is added to a base word, it is added with no spelling change in either the prefix or the base:

re- + spell = respell   mis- + spell = misspell

When a <u>suffix</u> is added to a base word, the spelling of the base word may change. Here are the rules that tell you when and how the spelling of the base changes:

If a word ends in y preceded by a consonant, change y to i before adding any suffix except a suffix that already begins with i:

happy + –ly = happily   beauty + –cian = beautician

If, however, a word ends in a y preceded by a vowel, or if the suffix begins with i, there is no spelling change.

boy + –like = boylike   baby + –ish = babyish

If a word ends with a silent e, (except for words ending with ce or ge), the e is dropped before suffixes beginning with a vowel. Keep the e before all other suffixes.

notice + –ing = noticing   notice + –able = noticeable

If a word ends with a ce or a ge, the e is dropped only before a suffix beginning with e or i.

manage + –ed = managed   manage + –able = manageable

If a one–syllable word consists of the letter combination consonant–vowel–consonant (CVC), the final consonant is doubled before adding a suffix beginning with a vowel. Do not double the final consonant before a suffix beginning with a consonant. (Exceptions: words ending with x or w.)

war + –ing = warring   BUT: tow + –ing = towing

110

If a word of more than one syllable ends with CVC, it follows the consonant–doubling rule stated above if the last syllable of the base word is stressed when the suffix is added.

prefer + –ed = preferred
prefer + –ment = preferment   (no doubling; suffix begins with a consonant)

prefer + –ence = preference ⎫ (no doubling; stress does not fall
alter + –ation = alteration ⎬ on last syllable of base + suffix)

46 Summary & Review: Plurals

The plural of most English nouns is formed by adding –s to the singular: *dogs*, *books*, *elephants*.

Nouns ending in *s*, *z*, *ch*, *sh*, or *x*, add –es to form the plural:

    bosses   buzzes   watches   dishes   foxes

Nouns ending in a consonant + *y* change *y* to *i* and add –es.
Nouns ending in a vowel + *y* simply add –s with no spelling change:

    baby, babies   lady, ladies   try, tries
    boy, boys   monkey, monkeys   tray, trays

Many, but not all, nouns ending in consonant plus *o* add –es to form the plural. You will probably need to check a dictionary to be sure.

    echo, echoes   potato, potatoes   **BUT**: silo, silos

Nouns ending in a vowel + *o*, and most proper nouns and musical terms ending in a consonant + *o*, simply add an –s:

    radio, radios   Filipino, Filipinos   piano, pianos

Certain nouns ending in *f* or *fe* change the *f* or *fe* ending to *v* and add –es. Others merely add an –s. Still others can form their plurals either way:

    knife, knives   chief, chiefs   dwarf, dwarfs *or* dwarves

Plurals of proper names are formed by adding –s or –es, with no spelling change in the name:

    Mr. Fox, the Foxes   Mr. Wolf, the Wolfs

Symbols, such as letters and mathematical signs, form the plural by adding an apostrophe plus –s:

a's   b's   x's   ÷'s

Troublesome compound nouns usually pluralize the first word of the compound:

mother–in–law, mothers–in–law

The –s (or –es) forms of the present tense of verbs are formed like plurals, except that verbs ending in f do not change f to v:

I wolf down my food.   He wolfs down his food.

47 Summary & Review: IE & EI

Put *i* before *e*:

    bel*ie*ve   ch*ie*f   qu*ie*t

Except after *c*:

    dec*ei*ve   rec*ei*pt   c*ei*ling

Or when sounded like *a*, as in *neighbor* and *weigh*:

    fr*ei*ght   n*ei*ghborhood   w*ei*ght

Exceptions:

N*ei*ther l*ei*sured for*ei*gn sh*ei*k s*ei*zed th*ei*r w*ei*rd h*ei*ght as forf*ei*t for th*ei*r h*ei*fers' prot*ei*n, O Sh*ei*la and N*ei*l.

A financ*ie*r is a spec*ie*s of sc*ie*ntist.

114

48 Summary & Review: Homophones

Here is a list of homophones and frequently confused words discussed in the Lesson Book:

Homophones containing a confusing spelling of a long vowel:

brake, break	die, dye	plain, plane
stake, steak	right, write	waste, waist
steel, steal	whole, hole	real, reel

Homophones containing confusing spellings of an unaccented syllable:

affect, effect	capital, capitol	principal, principle
accept, except	miner, minor	stationary, stationery

Homophones in some dialects but not in others:

formerly, formally	wheather, whether	poor, pour, pore
quite, quiet, quit	clothes, close, cloths	

Words that are not strictly homophones but that are frequently confused:

advise, advice	choose, chose	passed, past
lead, led	loose, lose	desert, dessert

Homophones involving apostrophes:

its, it's	their, they're, there	whose, who's
your, you're	theirs, there's	

Phrase and number homophones and confusing words:

all ready, already	four, for	two, to, too
all together, altogether	fourth, forth	
all right	forty	

49 Summary & Review: Apostrophes

Add an apostrophe plus –s to form the **possessive** of singular nouns:

    dog's   grass's   book's   Bill's   Mr. Jones's

If a singular noun already ends in s and has more than one syllable, you may choose to form its possessive with an apostrophe alone:

    Jesus' name   goodness' sake   Archimedes' principle

To form the **plural possessive** of any noun, first form the plural. If the plural ends in s, simply add an apostrophe to form the **possessive**. If the plural does not end in s, add an apostrophe plus –s:

    dog, dogs, *dogs'*   Mr. Jones, the Joneses, *the Joneses'*
    man, men, *men's*

The possessive form of a personal pronoun does *not* contain an apostrophe:

    its hers yours theirs whose

The possessive form of an indefinite pronoun does contain an apostrophe:

    anyone's   everybody's   someone's

An apostrophe replaces any missing letters in a **contraction**:

    I + am = I'm   he + is = he's   let + us = let's

Be, have, do, and the helping verbs *will, would, should, can, could,* and *must* frequently contract with *not*:

    isn't   don't   haven't won't   can't   mustn't
    hasn't didn't hadn't   wouldn't couldn't

Nouns and pronouns often contract with *be, have, will* and *would*:

    he's (*he is* or *he has*)   he'd (*he had* or *he would*)
    you're they're   they've I'm we'll who's

50 Summary & Review: Capitalization

The following types of words are usually spelled with capitals:

Personal names, nicknames, initials:

John Doe   Alfred Q. Katzenellen   "Bad News" Bascomb

Titles of respect when they precede a name, or when they are used as nouns of address:

Dr. Nuñez   General Puntz   Mr. Dolfini

Titles of honor, nobility, or high office (but not ordinary titles) when they are used in place of a person's name:

The President is in conference with the Secretary of State.

Words showing relationship, when not preceded by words like *my* or *the*:

If Mother and Dad visit my uncle, they will take me with them.

Place names, or names of regions:

New York   Mississippi River   English Channel   the South

Names of organizations, political bodies, religions, etc.:

the Red Cross   the Senate   Christianity

Proper adjectives (but not the words they modify):

the Christian religion   the American flag   Italian bread

Days of the week, names of months, and holidays:

Sunday   February   Thanksgiving Day

Brand names:

Ajax   Coke   Kleenex   Chevrolet

Names of historical events, periods, wars, and battles:

The Civil War   The Age of Exploration   Colonial Era

The first and last words of the titles of books, stories, plays, etc., and other words in the title, except short prepositions, conjunctions, and words like *a, an,* or *the*:

Alice in Wonderland   *To the Lighthouse*

51 Summary & Review: Spelling & the Dictionary

The dictionary gives the following special spelling information about each entry:

> Whether or not it is capitalized.
> Whether or not it contains a hyphen.
> Whether it consists of one or more than one word.

Every word of more than one syllable is entered in the dictionary with a space (or a dot, or a very small dash) between syllables. In your writing, whenever you hyphenate a word at the end of a line, the break should occur between syllables. For example, the word *exaggeration* might be hyphenated in any of the following ways:

exag– geration	exagger– ation	ex– aggeration	exaggera– tion

The grammatical forms listed below may not have main entries in a dictionary. Instead, they may be listed before or after the definitions of the main entry word from which they are formed:

> Noun plurals (*dog—dogs*)
> Verb participles and past tense (*go, going, gone*)
> *–er* and *–est* forms of adjectives (*bigger, biggest*)
> Suffixed forms (*craftily, craftiness,* from *crafty*)

If you wish spelling information on one of these, you may have to look up the main entry of the word from which they are formed.

A word may have two spellings, like *ax* and *axe*. Both spellings will be listed in the dictionary. In your own writing, if you do not know which spelling to use, choose the first spelling of the main entry that has a full definition after it, because this spelling is usually considered the most correct.

A special chart in the front matter of your dictionary lists various ways in which common English sounds are spelled. The chart is usually called something like *Common Spellings of English,* or *Spelling Chart.* It may be included as part of a pronunciation guide.

This chart may be useful when you wish to look up a word whose spelling you are unsure of. In addition, here are a few pointers to keep in mind:

A consonant in the middle of a word is often doubled if it comes after a short vowel (*hopping, fatter*).

The schwa sound (the sound of the unstressed vowel in a word like *places* or *circus*) is usually spelled with a single vowel. Exceptions: *–ous* and *–ain* in words like *famous* and *mountain.*

Some unusual spellings, such as the *ough* combination, can be pronounced several different ways (*through, though, rough, ought*).

Short vowels are more often spelled the way they sound than long vowels are.

Long vowel sounds are often made up of two–letter combinations (as in *aim*). A word with a long vowel in the last syllable is often spelled with a final silent *e* (*hope, decide*).

J
MASTERY TESTS

52

Mastery Test:
Prefixes & Suffixes

Write the words formed by the following combinations of prefixes and base words or of base words and suffixes.

1. dis– + similar _____
2. un– + noticed _____
3. mis– + spell _____
4. pad + –ed _____
5. manage + –ment _____
6. decide + –ing _____
7. swim + –er _____
8. damage + –ing _____
9. confer + –ence _____
10. teach + –able _____
11. journey + –ed _____
12. begin + –ing _____
13. forget + –ful _____
14. mix + –er _____
15. rid + –ance _____
16. open + –er _____
17. lazy + –ness _____
18. occur + –ence _____
19. day + –ly _____
20. move + –able _____

53 Mastery Test: Plurals

Write the plurals of each of the following words or symbols.

1. piccolo _____
2. monkey _____
3. wife _____
4. chief _____
5. try _____
6. Gomes (a family name) _____
7. batch _____
8. alloy _____
9. wish _____
10. puppy _____
11. knife _____
12. ox _____
13. mother–in–law _____
14. + _____
15. 6 _____

In each of the following sentences, underline the correct verb form in the parentheses.

16. Jim (beliefs, believes) anything you tell him.
17. Rebecca (wolfs, wolves) down her food.
18. Nora (defys, defies) her parents.
19. Edwin (destroys, destroies) my plans.
20. Eric (mans, men) the lifeboat.

Mastery Test: IE & EI

Copy the words suggested below, supplying *ie* or *ei* in place of the dashes.

1. h--ght _____
2. p--ce _____
3. br--f _____
4. dec--ve _____
5. for--gn _____
6. fr--ght _____
7. misch--f _____
8. c--ling _____
9. s--ze _____
10. w--ght _____

55 Mastery Test: Homophones

Below are twenty definitions, each followed by two or three words in parentheses. Underline the word in parentheses that best fits the definition before it.

1. The head of a school   (principal, principle)
2. Number 4 in order   (forth, fourth)
3. OK   (alright, all right)
4. By now   (already, all ready)
5. Belonging to it   (its, it's)
6. Belonging to them   (their, there, they're)
7. Past tense of the verb *pass*   (passed, past)
8. Not tight   (lose, loose)
9. To suggest   (advice, advise)
10. Past tense of the verb *lead*   (led, lead)
11. Not rich   (pore, pour, poor)
12. A word used in making comparisons   (than, then)
13. Not fake   (real, reel)
14. To snap in two   (break, brake)
15. To influence   (affect, effect)
16. To receive   (accept, except)
17. What you wear   (close, clothes, cloths)
18. To leave or abandon   (desert, dessert)
19. If   (weather, whether)
20. The number 40   (forty, fourty)

56 Mastery Test: Apostrophes

In the blank space after each of the following words, write its possessive form.

1. mouse _____
2. it _____
3. someone _____
4. who _____
5. Mr. Harris _____

Write the *plural* possessive of each of the following words.

6. mouse _____
7. Harris _____
8. fox _____
9. goose _____
10. mind _____

Write the contractions indicated below.

11. can + not _____
12. let + us _____
13. she + is _____
14. she + has _____
15. you + would _____

In the following sentences, underline the word in parentheses that belongs in the sentence.

16. I think (its, it's) time to start.
17. They put on (there, their, they're) coats.
18. (Your, You're) expected to arrive before six.
19. She wants to know (whose, who's) responsible.
20. The responsibility is (there's, theirs).

Mastery Test: Capitalization

Capitalize each word in the following sentences that should be written with a capital letter. Write your capitals above the small letters.

1. The grocer suggested that mrs. simpson take the matter up with the president of the united states.

2. I'm certain we can cross the sahara desert if we just use some good old american know–how.

3. Last spring—on monday, may 12, to be exact—a swarm of maddened warblers attacked our house.

4. I had not expected to spend christmas aboard a raft in the bay of bengal.

5. Unfortunately, grandfather's mystery book *the case of the poisoned ear* appeared to be taken almost word for word from shakespeare's play *hamlet*.

6. Sullivan decided he wanted to practice druidism, the ancient religion of great britain.

7. I was terrified to learn that jim bascomb—better known as "bad news" bascomb—was going to be in my second grade class at the millard fillmore school.

8. The announcer held up a jar of a product known as fertz.

9. The doctor informed us that major general collins was sick with measles.

10. Peabody made the mistake of showing up at the boston tea party disguised as king george.

Mastery Test: Spelling & the Dictionary

Each of the following words contains a spelling mistake. Use your dictionary to find the correct spelling, and write it in the blank space after each word.

1. plentyful _____
2. fore arm _____
3. missionarys _____
4. ill–will _____
5. ill treat _____

Write the correct spellings of the following misspelled words in the blank after each word. Use your dictionary's spelling table as a guide, and look up each word in your dictionary to make sure you are spelling it correctly. Definitions for each word have been provided, to help you make sure you find the correct entry in the dictionary. (Misspellings are in the italicized portion of each word.)

6. *r*en (a kind of small bird) _____
7. *fl*ox (a kind of flower) _____
8. *sk*ooner (a sailing ship) _____
9. *ur*nest (*ur* as in *urge;* serious) _____
10. *ai*rudite (*ai* as in *air;* scholarly or learned) _____
11. ga*l*ant (noble or brave) _____
12. mi*shun* (errand, or special task) _____
13. p*i*kerel (a kind of fish) _____
14. s*ye* (rhymes with *eye;* to let out a deep breath) _____
15. *jahss*el (*ah* as in *shah;* to push roughly or to elbow aside) _____